DO'S & DON'TS
FASHION FLAT SKETCHING

SHIRTS
PANTS
SKIRTS
JACKETS
DRESSES

NICK VERREOS
DAVID PAUL

"Do's & Don'ts: Fashion Flat Sketching"

The "DO'S & DON'TS OF FASHION FLAT SKETCHING" is an indispensable guide for students of Fashion Design. This basic book serves as an introduction to proper sketching techniques when drawing pants, skirts, shirts and jackets.

Used as a companion to other instructional material on flat sketching, this supplemental guide does not replace the need for a formal textbook. Instead, it offers essential tips in completing your flat sketches properly.

We have identified key issues that are repeatedly made when it comes to Technical Flat Sketching. In an easy-to-read manner, this book shows both the CORRECT and INCORRECT ways of completing flat sketches in a simple Do's & Don'ts format.

BIOGRAPHY

Nick and David co-founded NIKOLAKI, in 2001. Their collections of upscale red carpet gowns and cocktail dresses have been worn by celebrities such as Beyoncé, Katy Perry, Heidi Klum, Eva Longoria and Carrie Underwood. NIKOLAKI has been carried in over 100 stores across the US and abroad.

Additionally, they design and produce NV Nick Verreos, a clothing line which has been available at Lord & Taylor, Dillard's and at major Home Shopping Networks.

Nick was the Winning Mentor of Project Runway: Under the Gunn and first received national and international attention after appearing on Project Runway. Nick is now a Consulting Producer on Bravo's Project Runway. He is a red carpet fashion expert and correspondent for various networks including E! Entertainment and ABC's "On The Red Carpet" LIVE from the Oscars.

Nick Received his Bachelor of Arts in Political Science at the University of California, Los Angeles/UCLA. He then continued on to the Fashion Institute of Design & Merchandising/FIDM, where he graduated from the Advanced Fashion Design Program.

As an educator, Nick has been an instructor at FIDM where he taught Fashion Sketching, Draping, Patternmaking and Design.

A native of Southern California, David Paul Attended the University of California, Los Angeles/UCLA where he received his Bachelor of Arts in Theatre Arts and subsequently, his MFA in Costume Design.

David went on to build an extensive resume in the world of entertainment and fashion styling for over 20 years. As a member of IATSE Local 705, David designed costumes and worked on shows such as "Queer Eye for the Straight Girl", "Passions", "Undressed" and numerous other productions for MTV, ABC, FOX, NIKELODEON and the WB.

David has also worked alongside Andre Leon Talley and Lisa Love for Vogue Magazine and with such illustrious photographers as Arthur Elgort, Regan Cameron, Noe DeWitt and Amanda DeCadanet, styling for Kate Hudson, Heidi Klum, Vanessa Paradis, Twiggy and Heather Graham.

Nick and David are Co-Chairs of Fashion Design, Advanced Fashion Design, Theatre Costume, and Film & TV Costume at the Fashion Institute of Design & Merchandising/FIDM. They also co-authored the best-selling book, "A Passion for Fashion", as well as "A Basic Guide To Pattern Drafting" and "A Comprehensive Guide To Men's Flat Sketching".

Published by NIKOLAKI PUBLISHING
© 2021 NIKOLAKI, INC.
Nick Verreos and David Paul assert their rights to
be identified as the authors of this work.

All rights reserved. No part of this publication my be
reproduced or transmitted in any form or by
any means electronic or mechanical, including
photocopy, recording or any information storage
and retrieval system without permission in
writing from the publisher.

TABLE OF CONTENTS

PANTS
- SEAMS 1
- PROPORTIONS 4
- ZIPPER TOPSTITCHING 5
- SHAPES 6

SKIRTS
- SLIT=SEAM 11
- DART LENGTH & WAIST SHAPE 12
- RUFFLES & GATHERS 13
- PLEATS 14
- SHAPES 15

SHIRTS/TOPS
- SHAPES 18
- COLLARS 20
- BUSTIER SHAPE & SLIT=SEAM 22
- CUFFS 23
- RIBBING 24

TABLE OF CONTENTS

- RIBBING & GATHERS..25

- COWL DRAPE..26

- STITCHING...27

DRESSES

- SEAMS..30

- RUFFLES, GATHERS & SHAPE..................................31

- SHAPE & SEAMS...33

JACKETS

- LAPELS & DARTS...36

- SHAPE & SEAMS...38

- HOODS..40

Pants
SEAMS

1. Always Draw a Center Front Seam

Don't

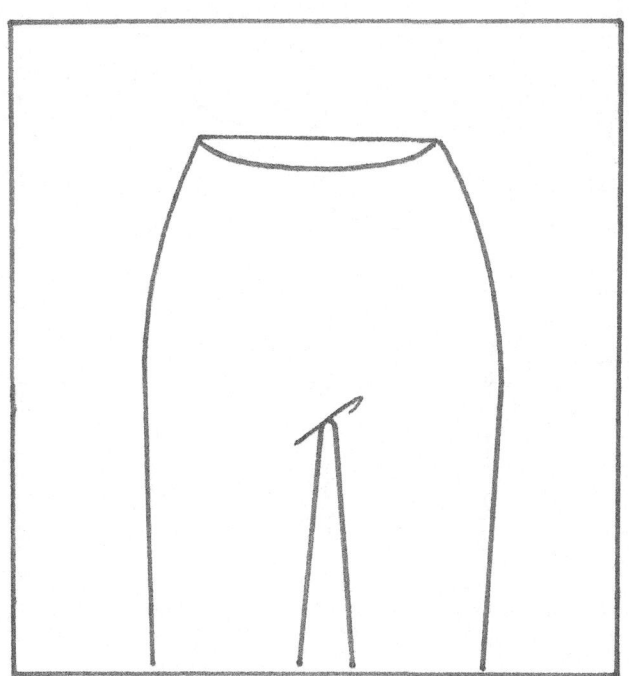

Do

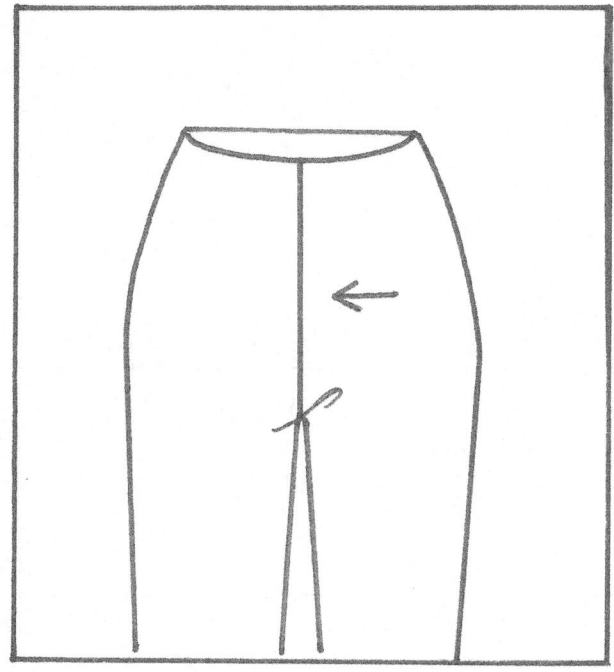

2. Always Draw a Center Back Seam

Don't

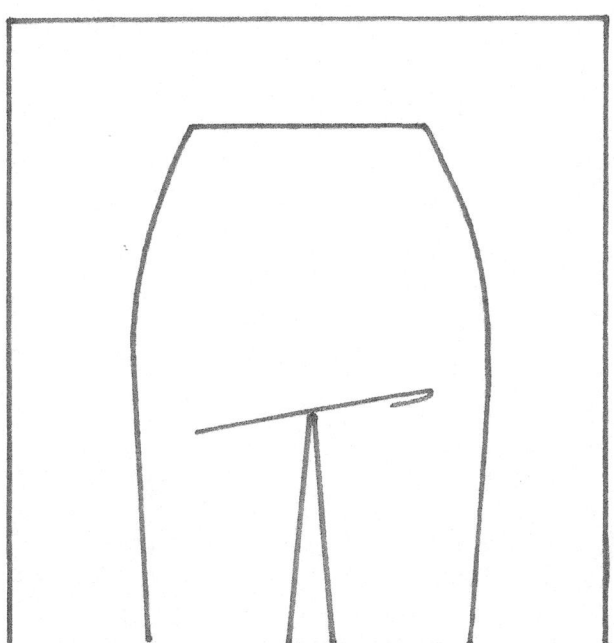

Do

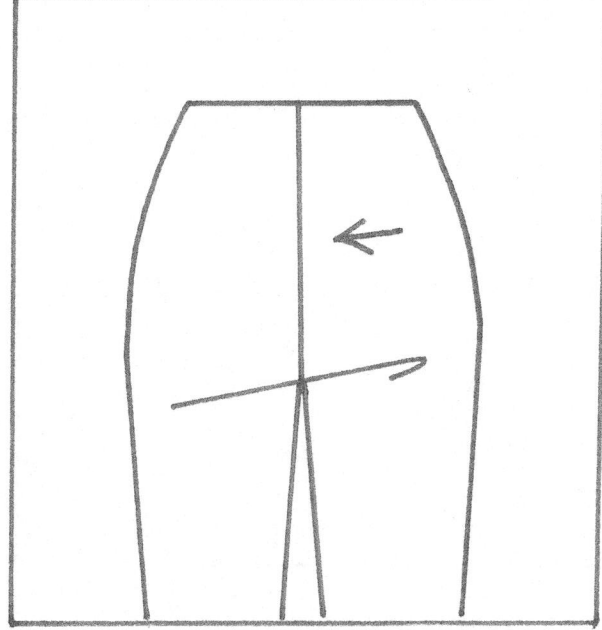

Pants
SEAMS

3. How to signify a FRONT CROTCH in a Flat Sketch:

Don't

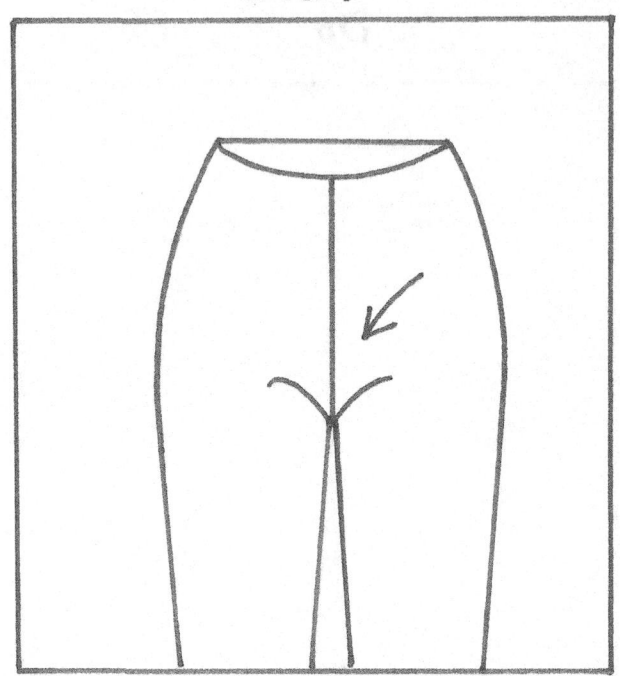

Do

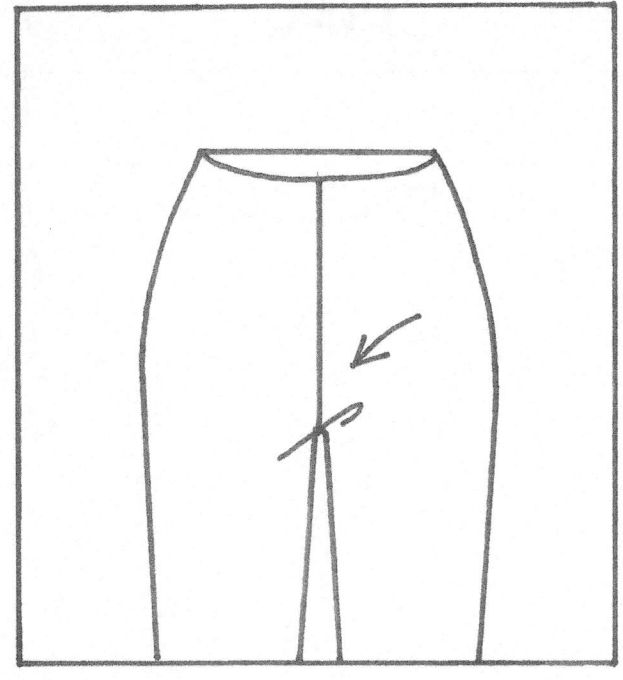

4. How to signify a BACK CROTCH in a Flat Sketch:

Don't

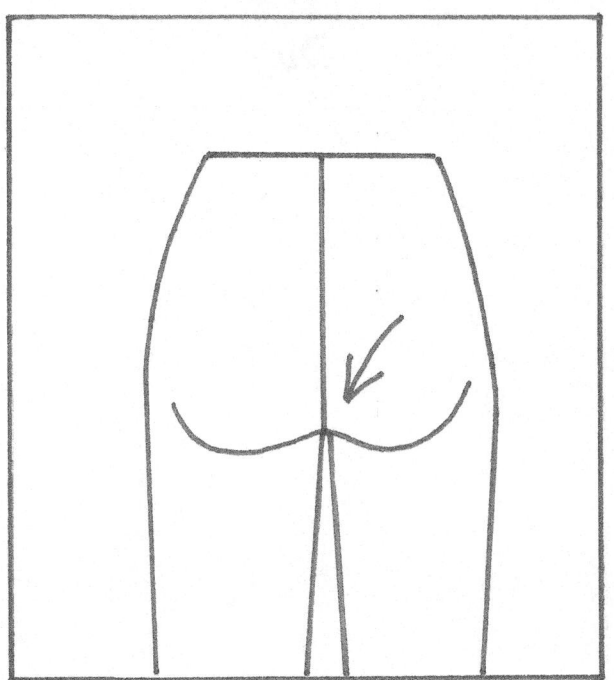

Do

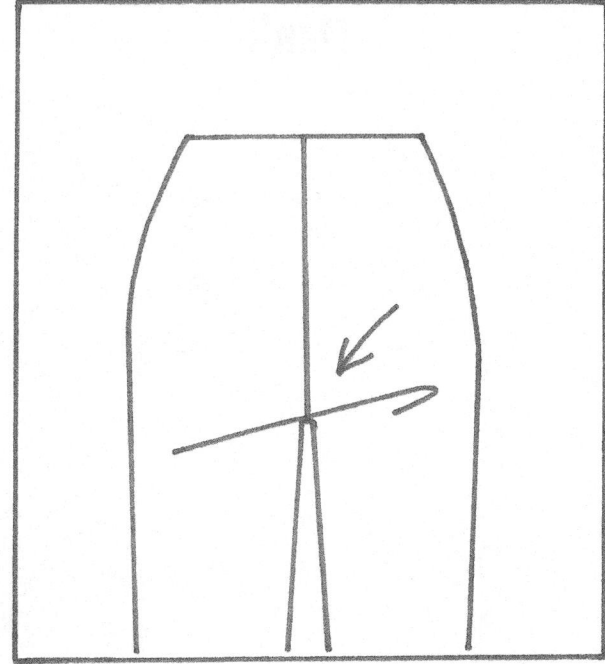

Pants
SEAMS

5. ZIPPER-SEAM: Any Time there is a ZIPPER there has to be a SEAM

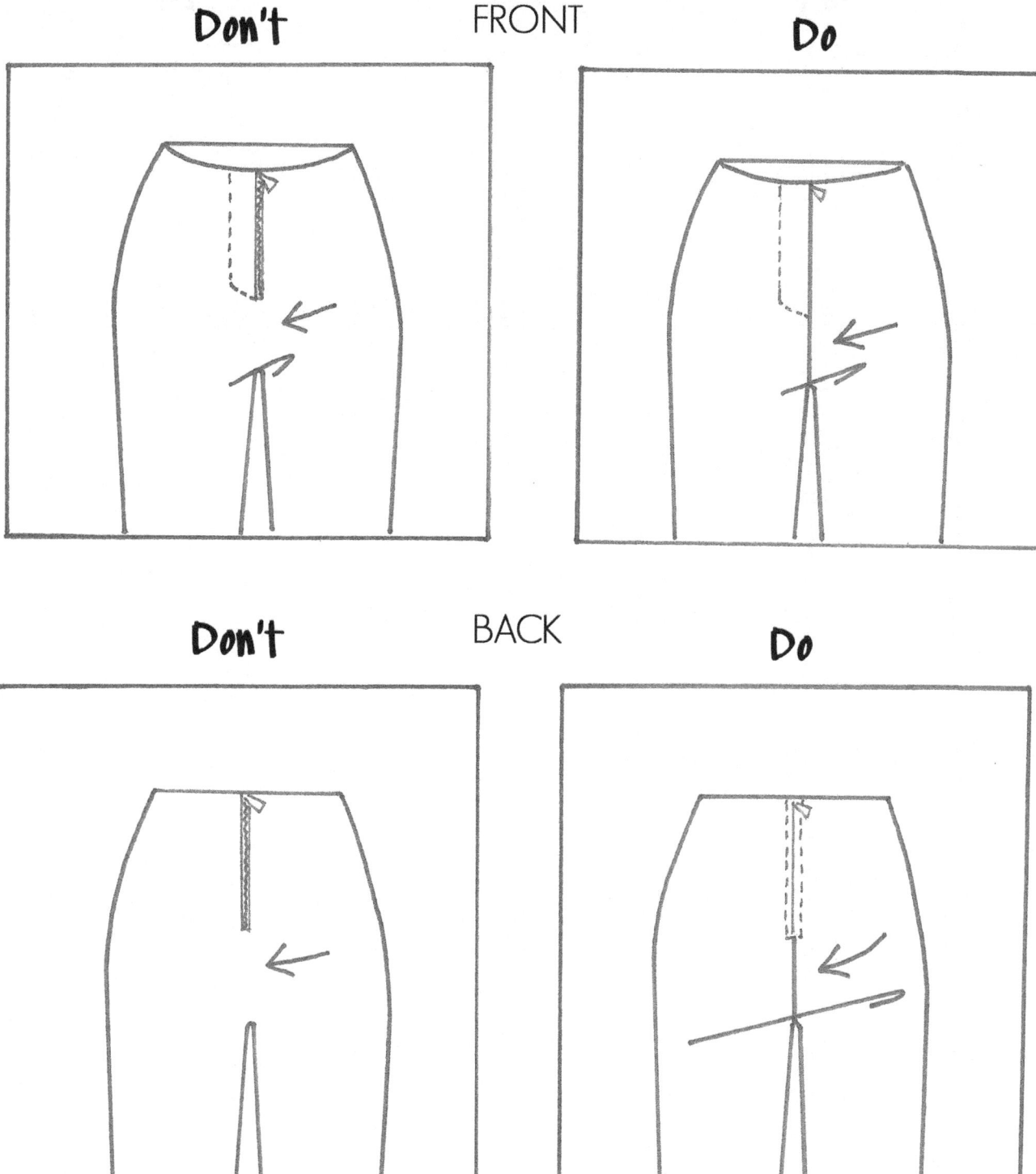

Pants
PROPORTIONS

6. Please Keep the 9-Head Rule when drawing LENGTHS of Pants, so you achieve the proper length

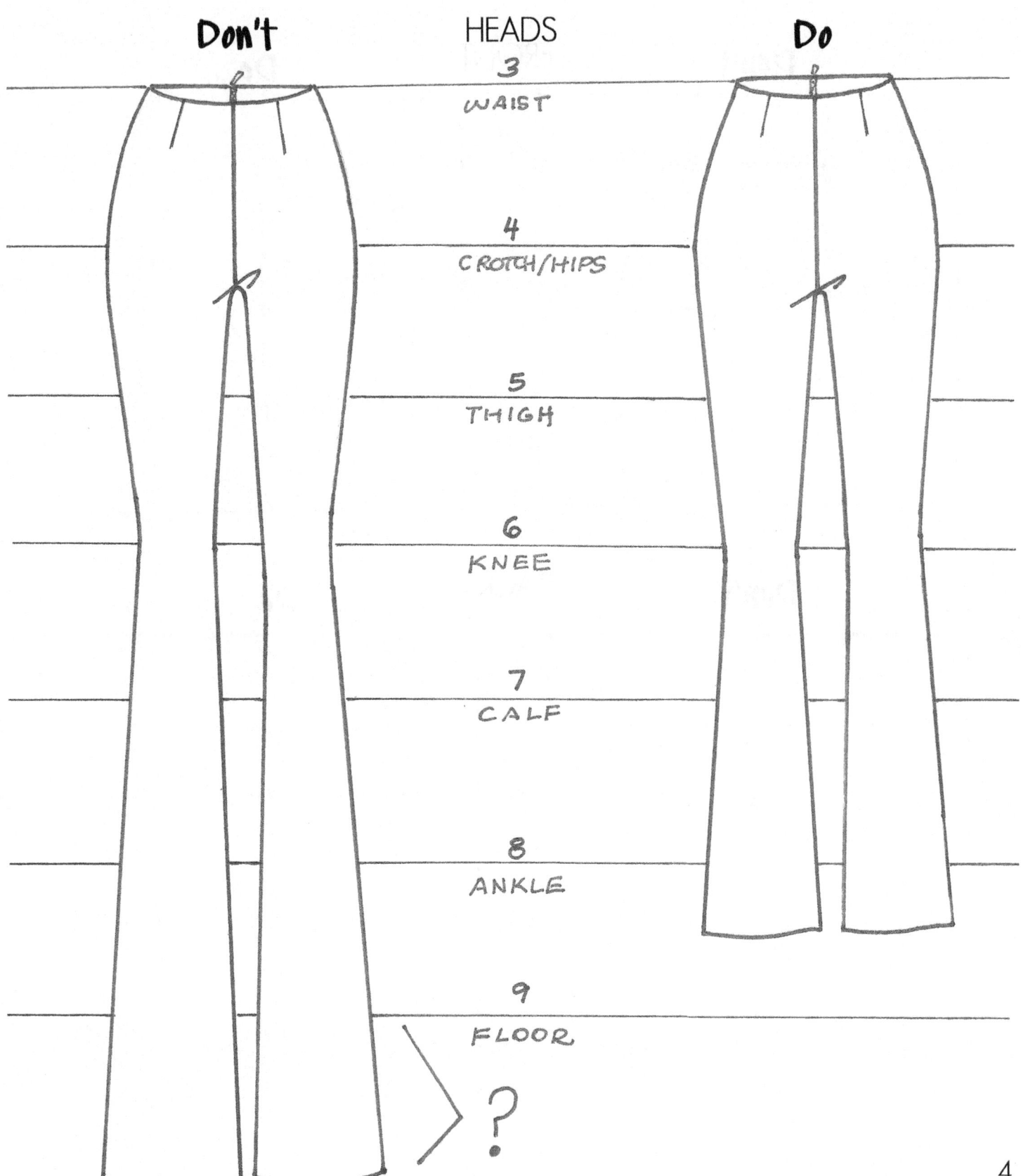

4.

Pants
ZIPPER TOPSTITCHING

Don't · Do

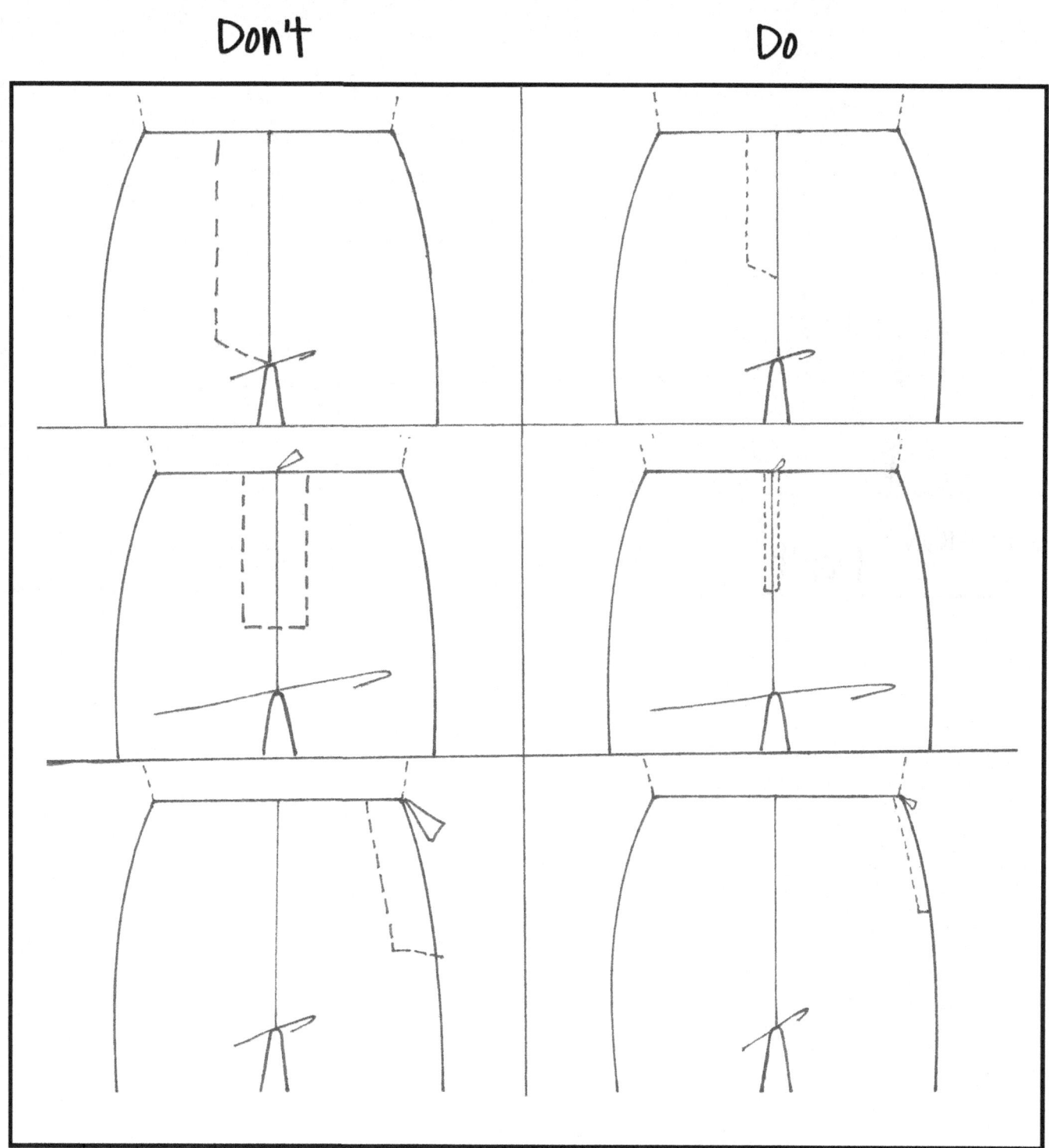

Pants
SHAPES

LEGGINGS:

Don't

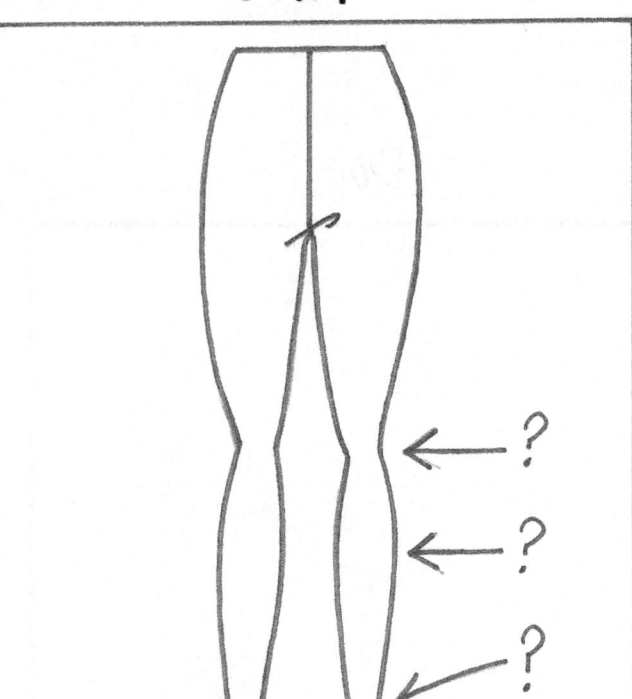

Do

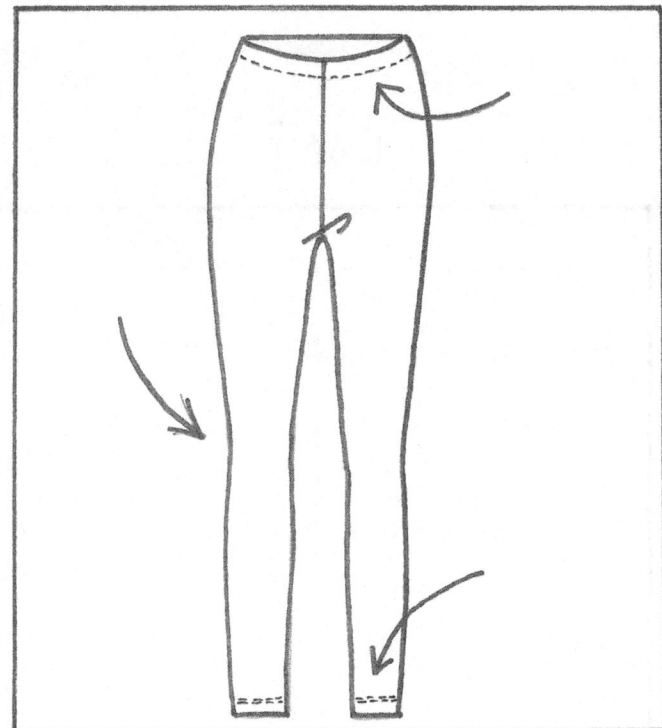

BELL BOTTOMS:

Don't

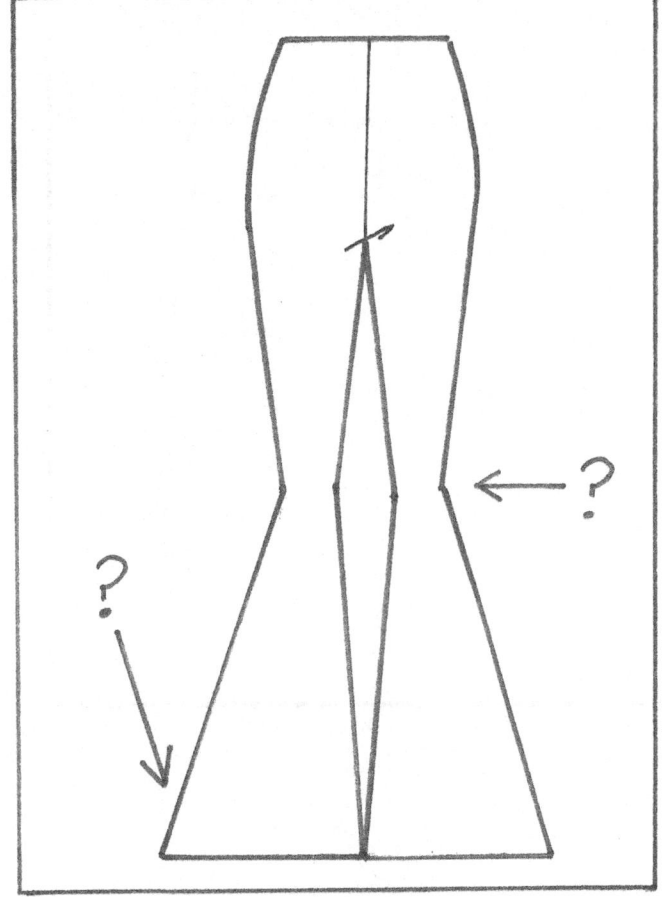

Do

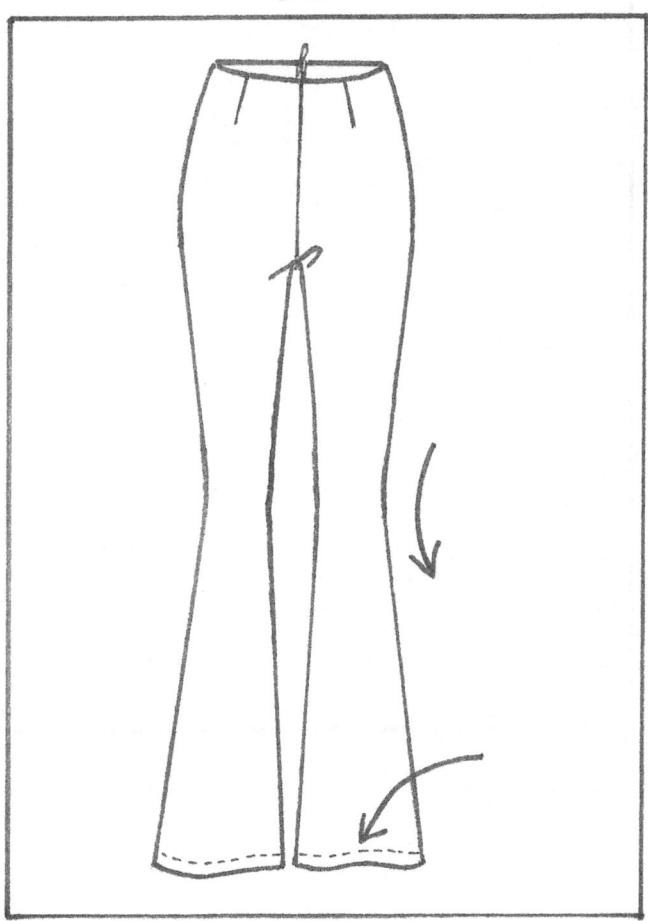

6.

Pants
SHAPES

CUFFS:

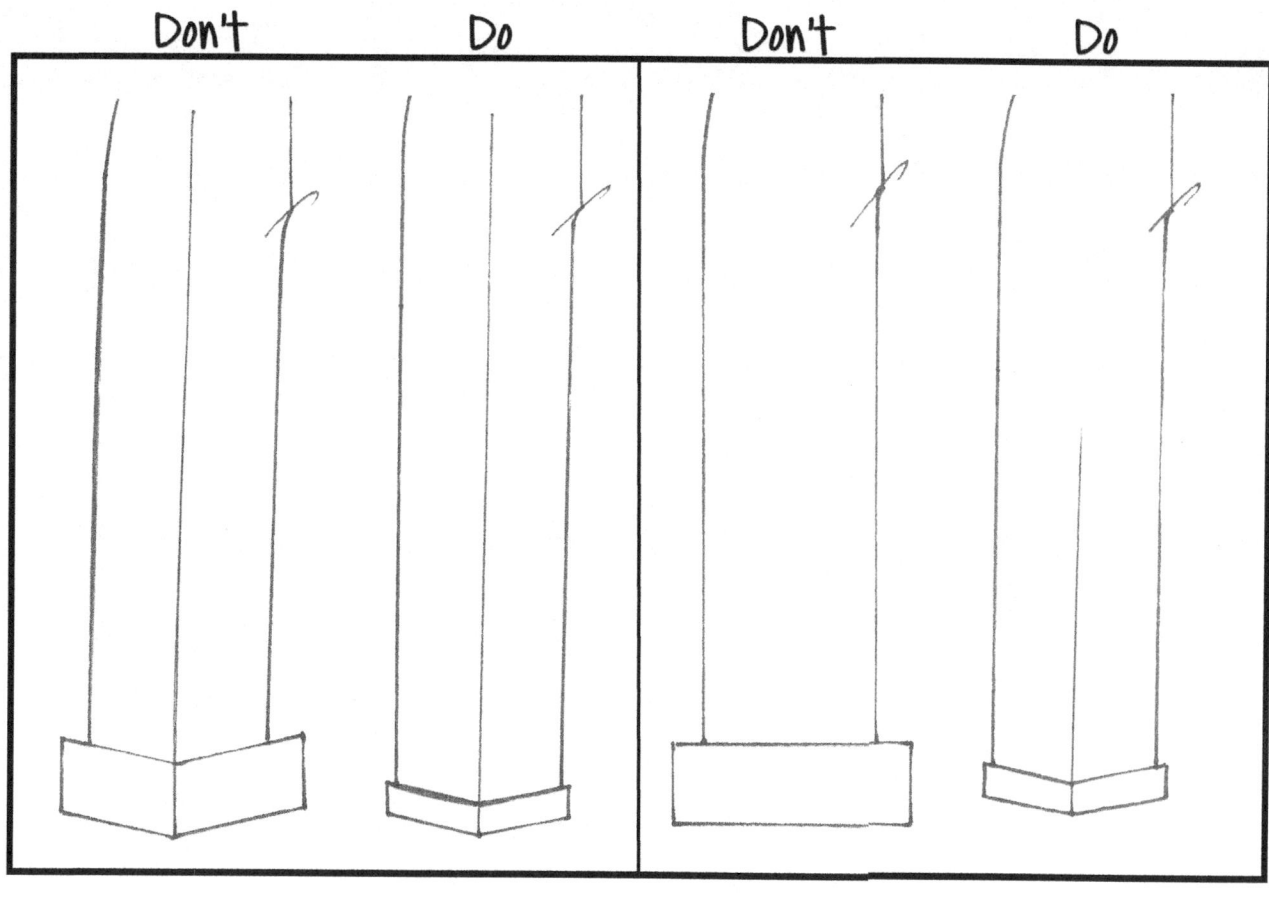

SHORTS:

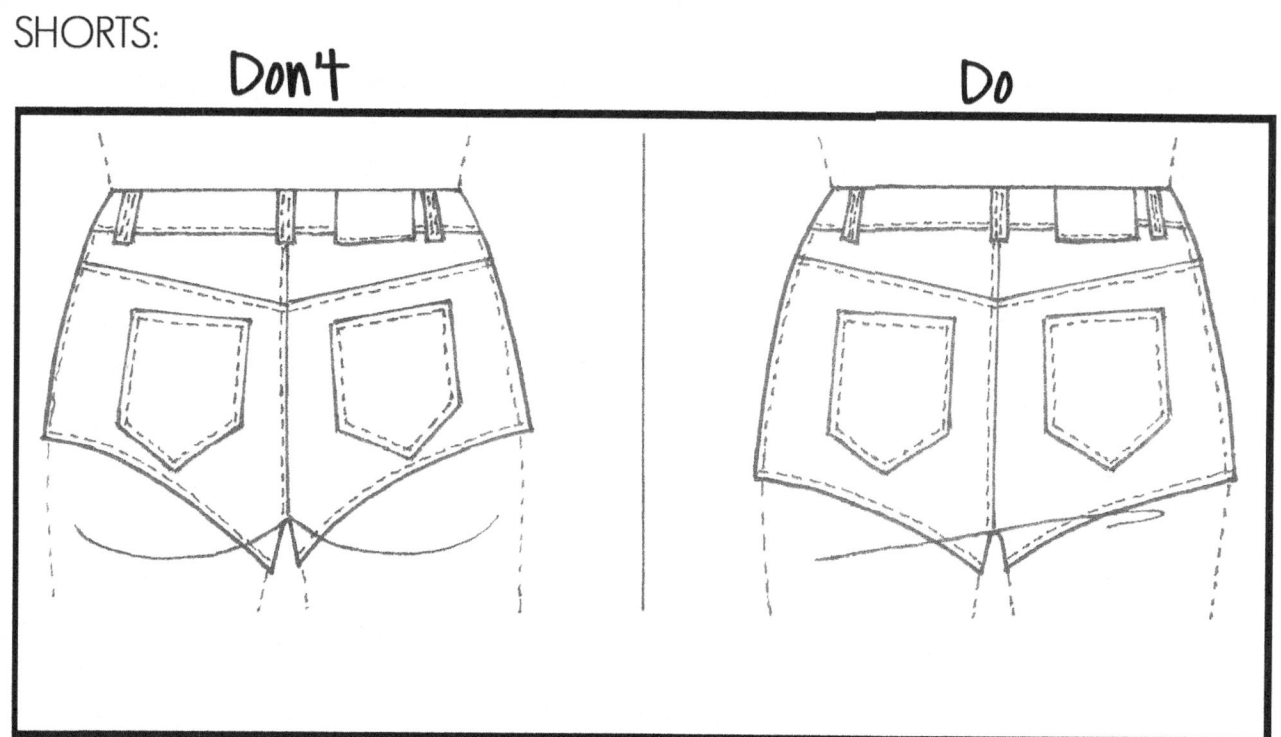

SKIRTS

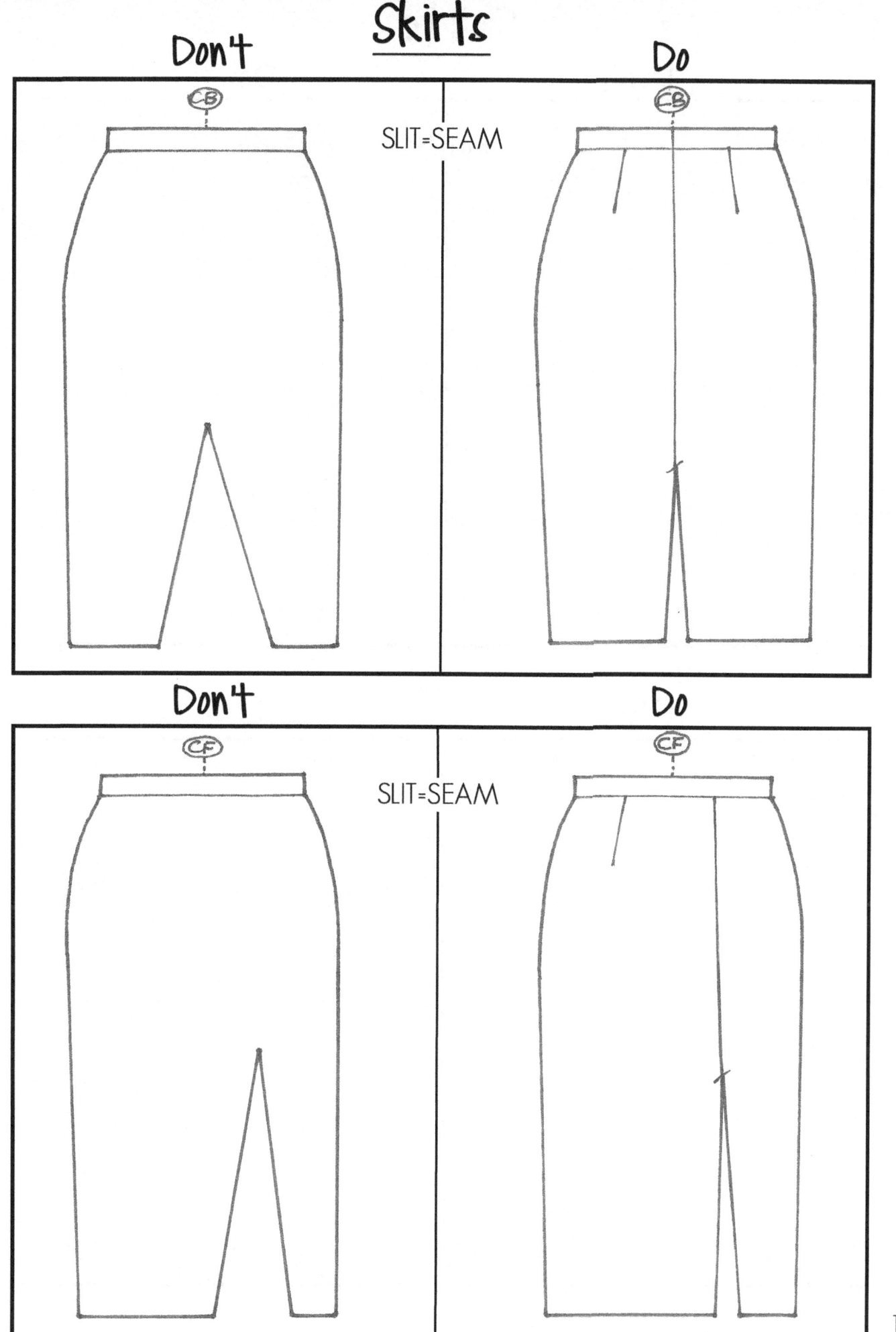

Skirts

Don't Do

DART LENGTH

Don't Do

WAIST SHAPE

Skirts

Don't	Do
RUFFLES	

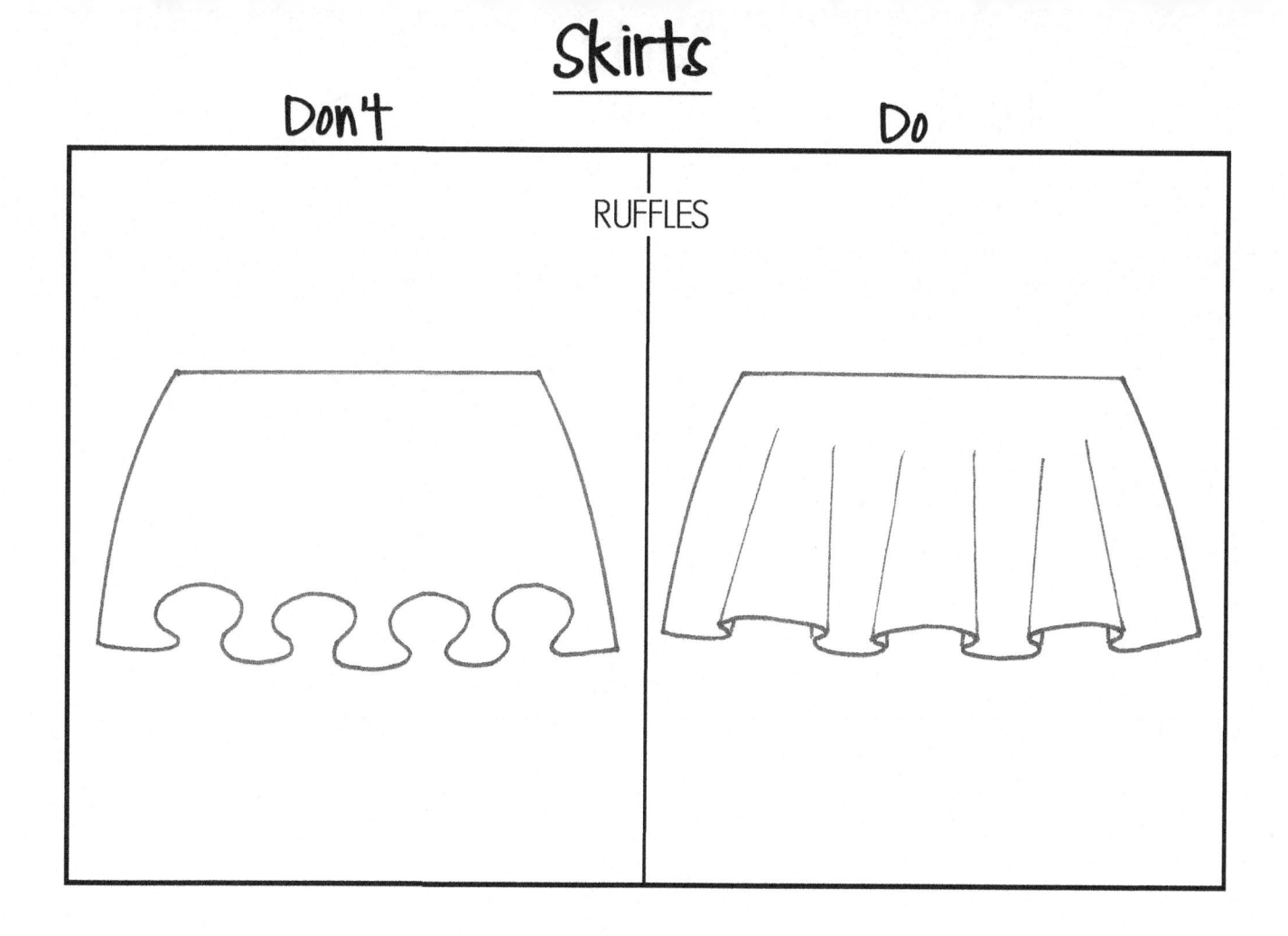

Don't	Do
GATHERS	

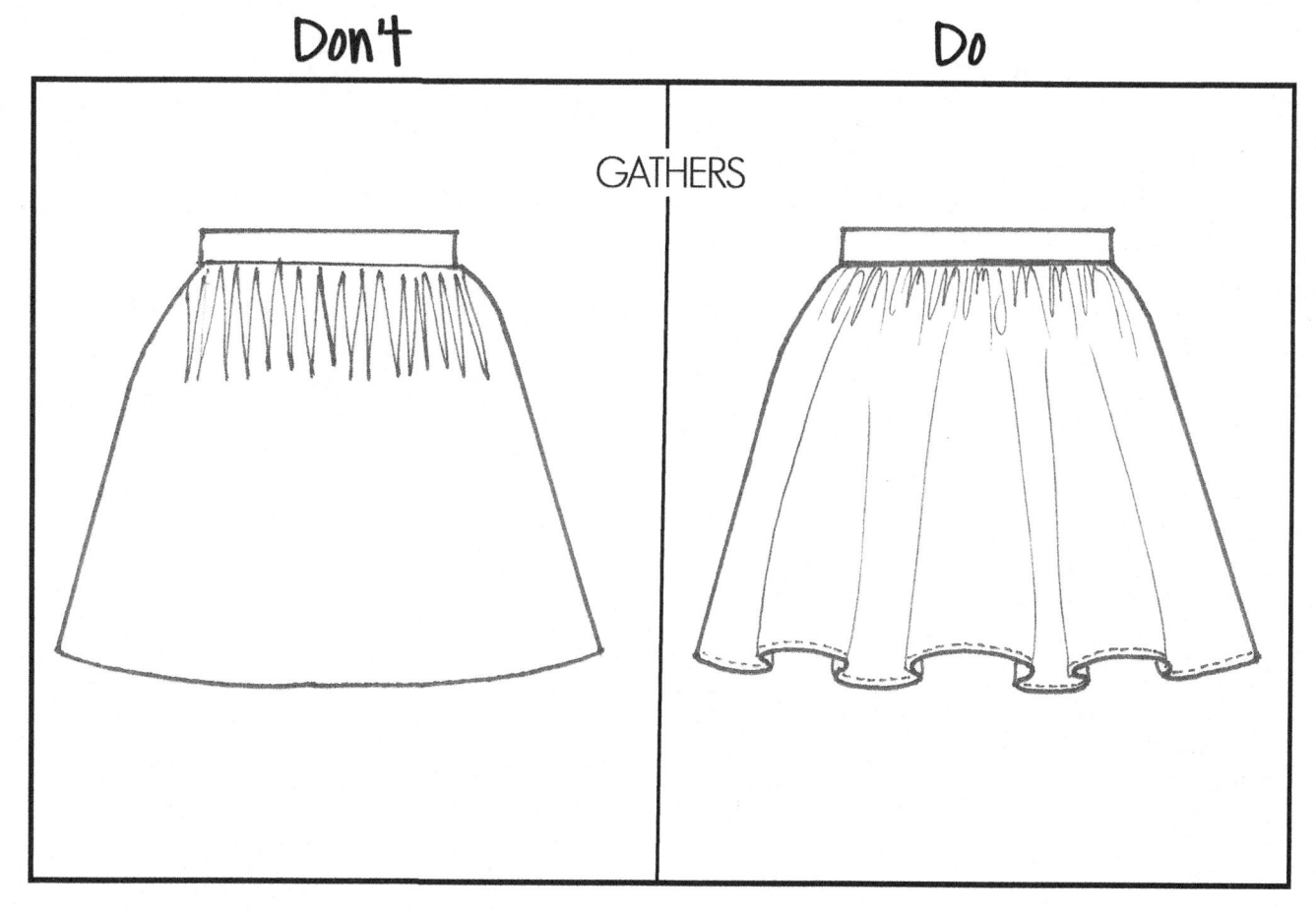

13.

Skirts
PLEATS

Don't
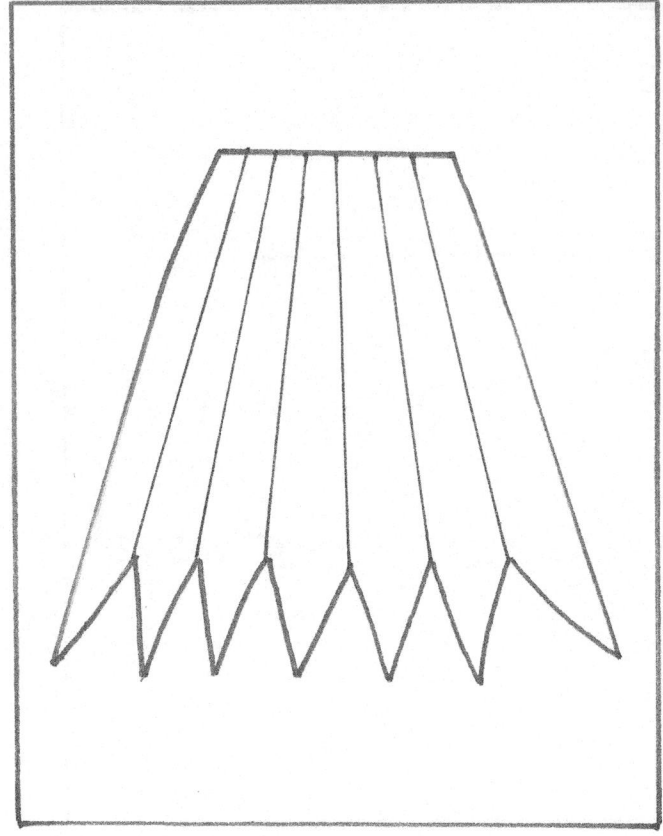

Do

Don't

Do

14.

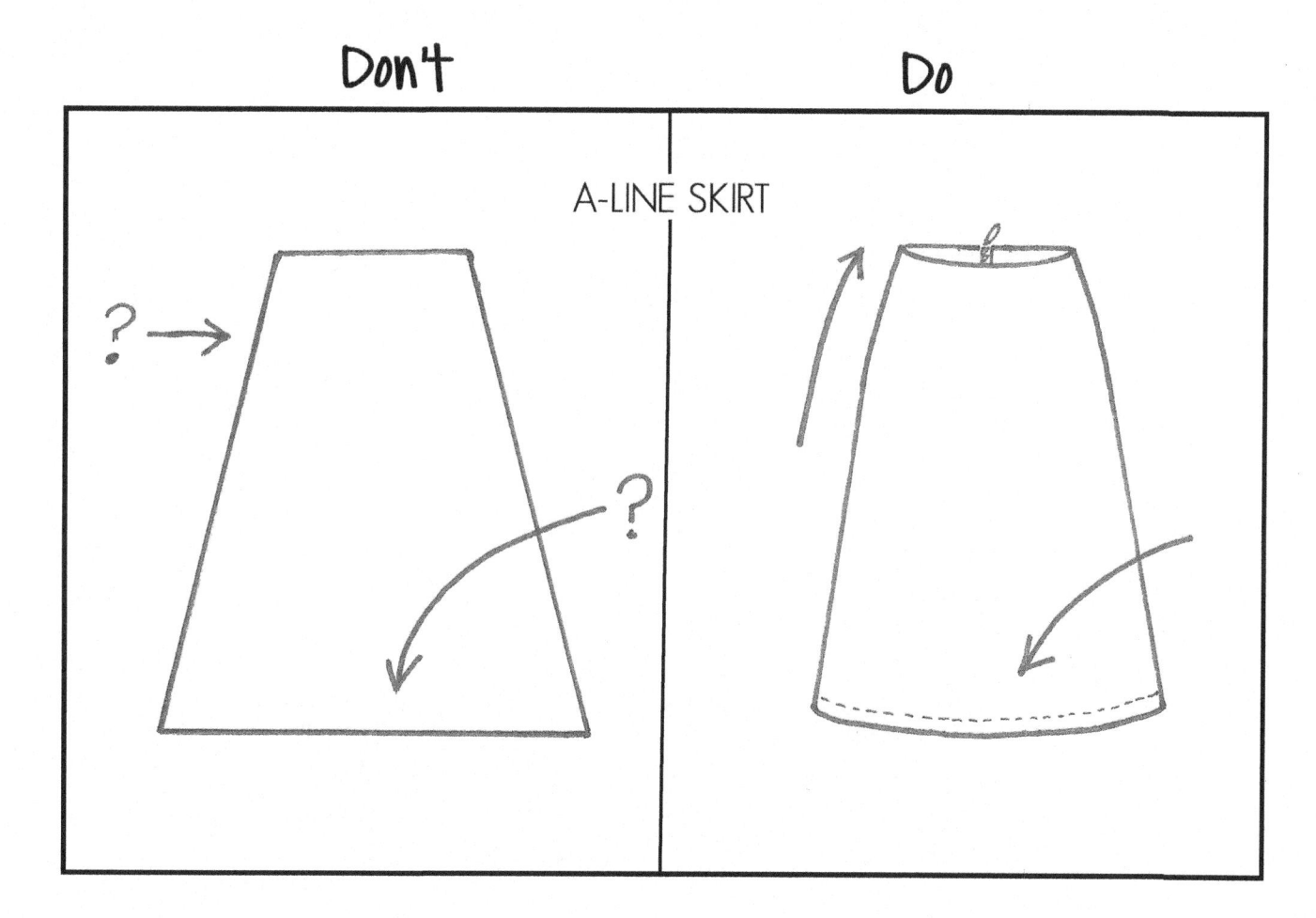

Skirts

Don't | Do

FULL SKIRT

Don't | Do

A-LINE SKIRT

Shirts
SHAPES

Don't

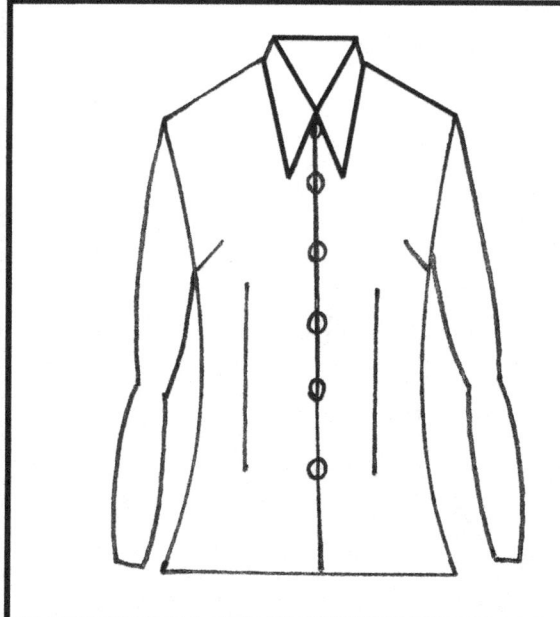

Do

Shirts
SHAPES

Don't   **Do**

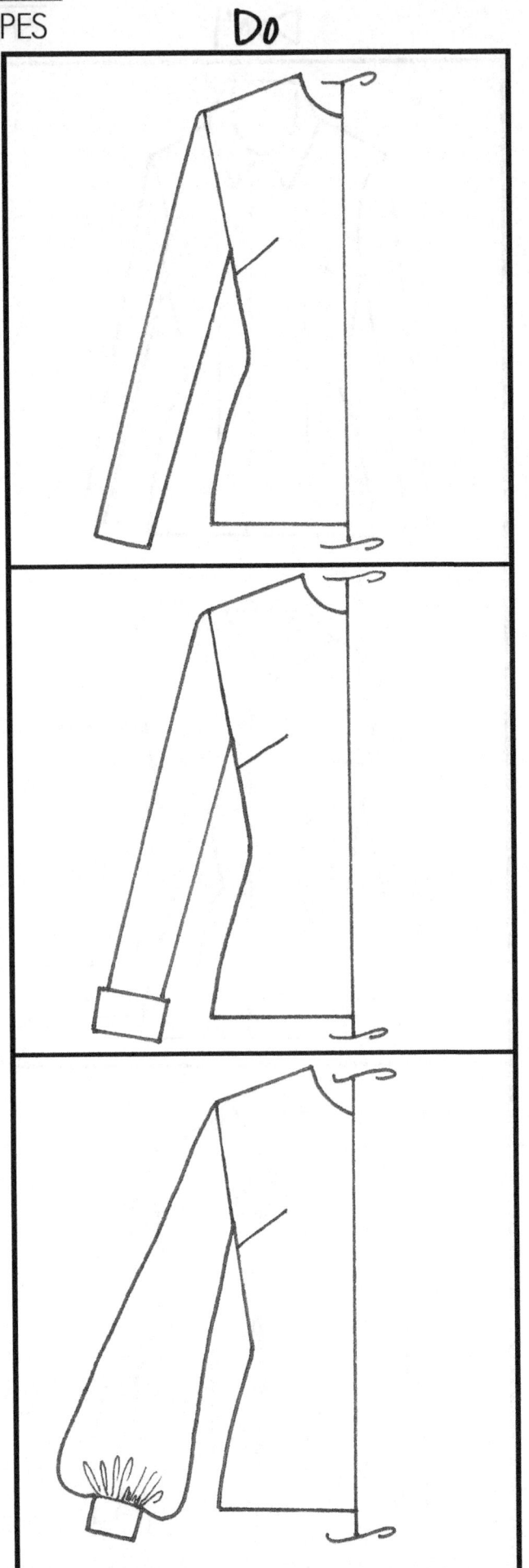

20.

Shirts
COLLARS

Always draw the INNER COLLAR seam line:

Don't

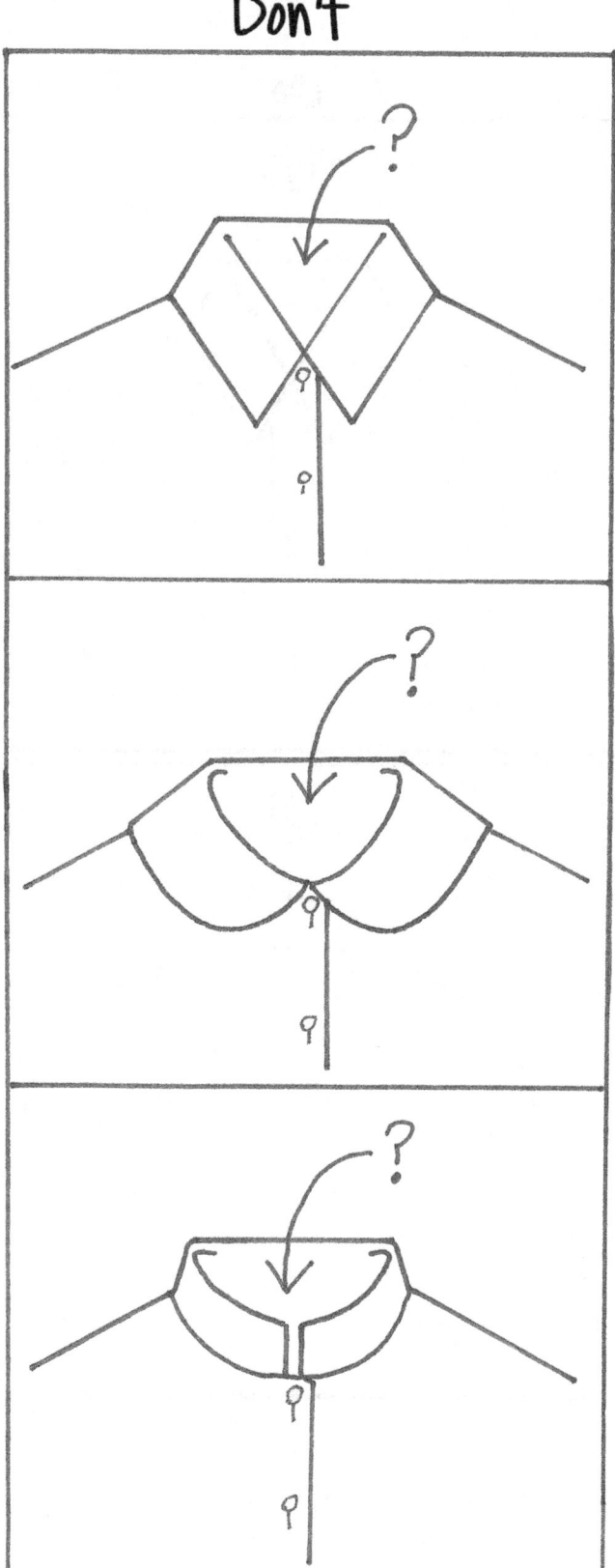

Do

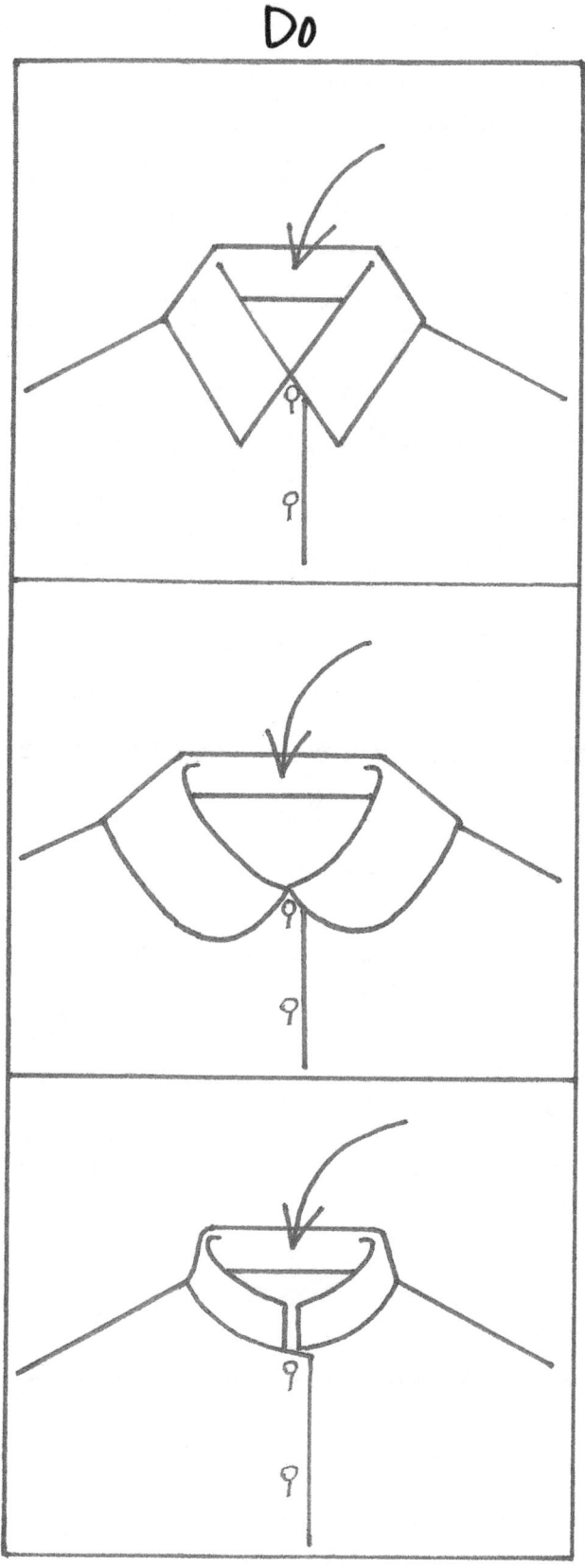

Shirts
COLLARS

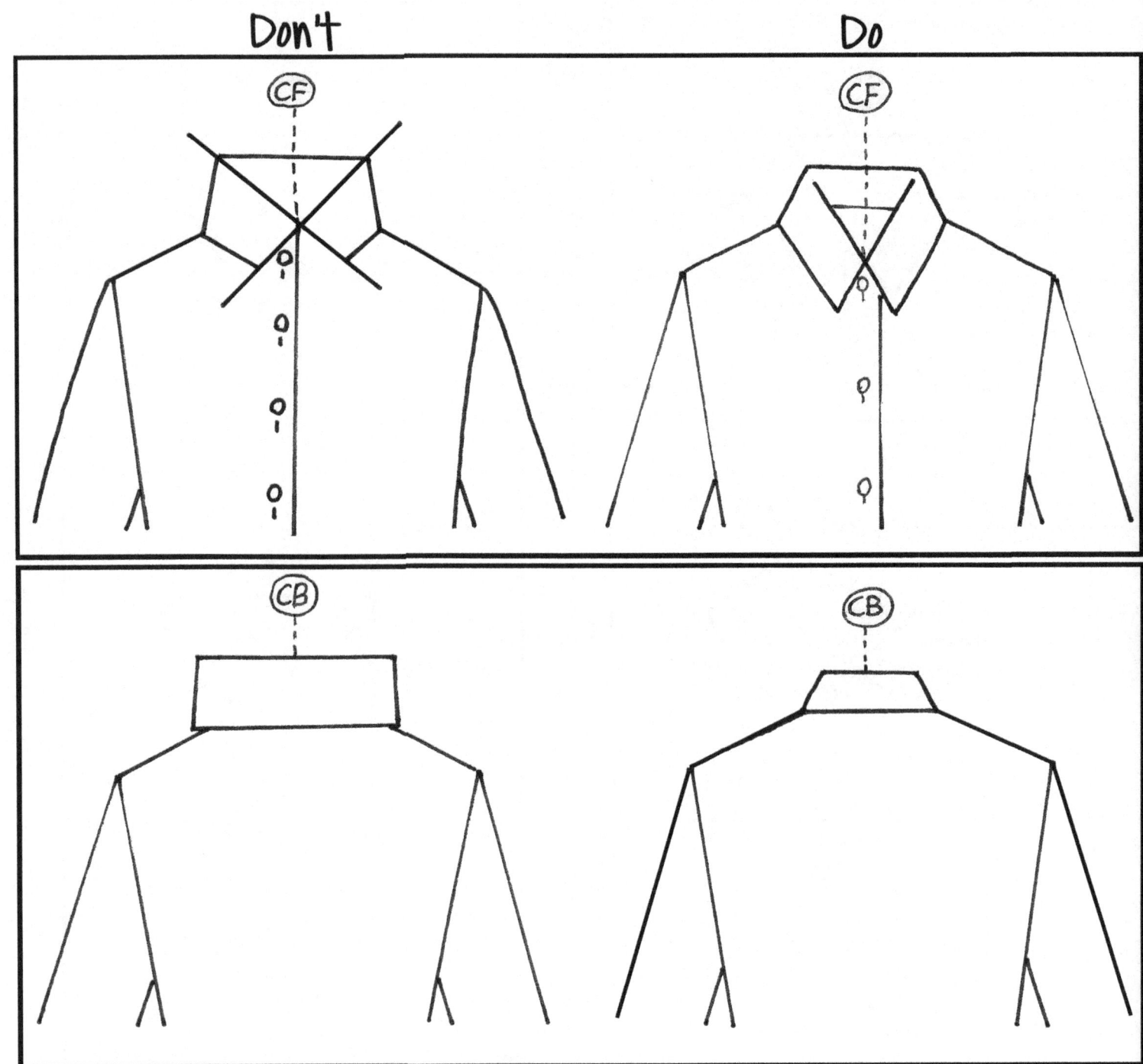

TOPS

BUSTIER SHAPE:

Don't | Do

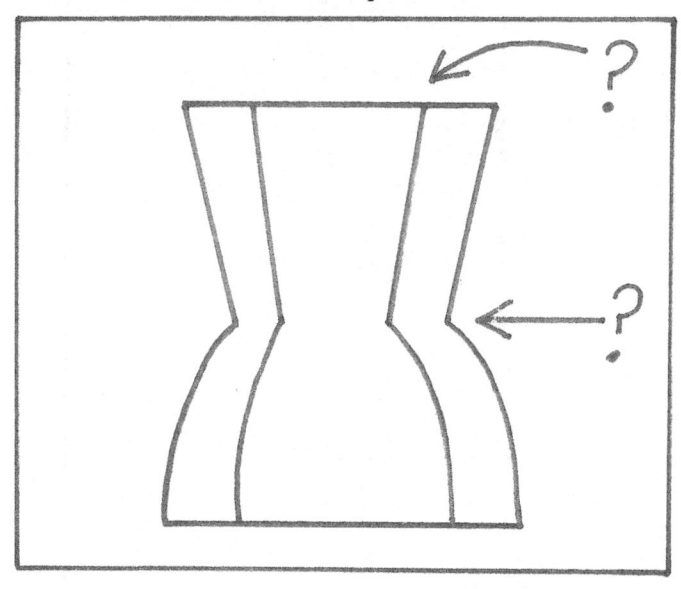

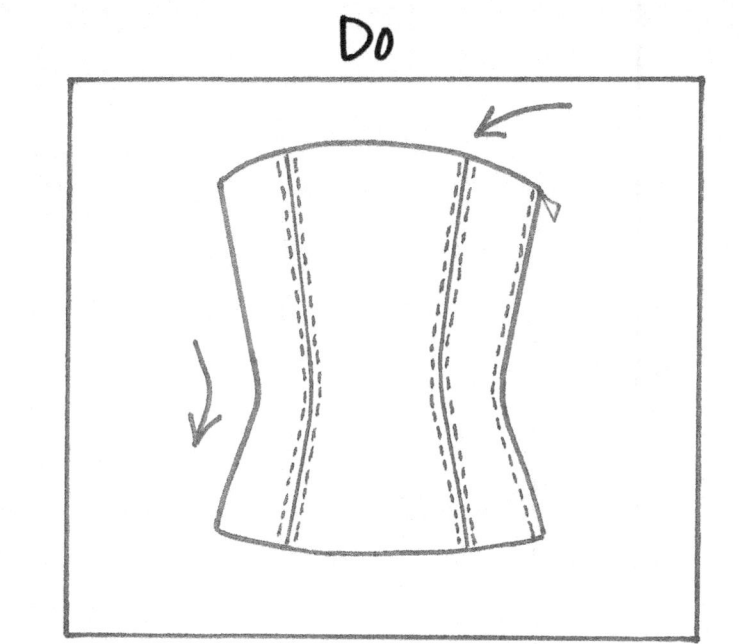

SLIT=SEAM:

Don't | Do

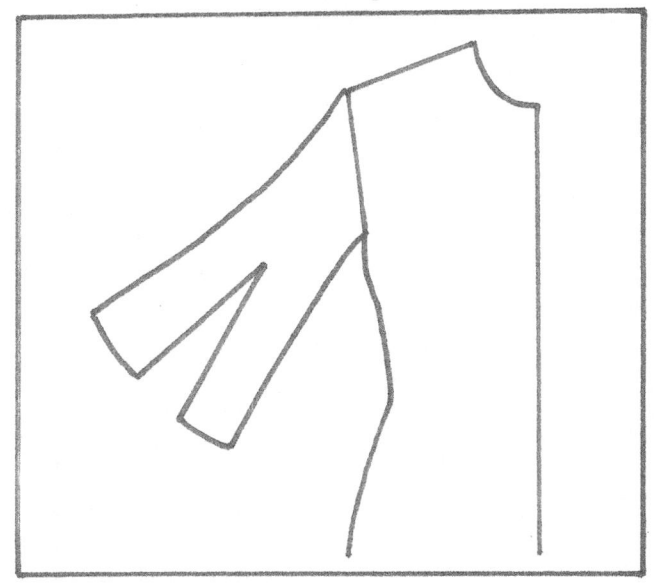

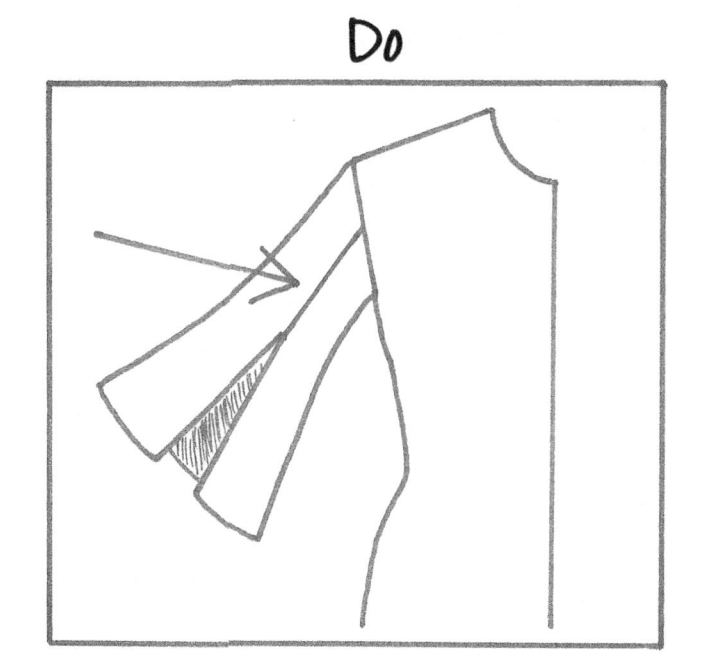

23.

Shirts
CUFFS:

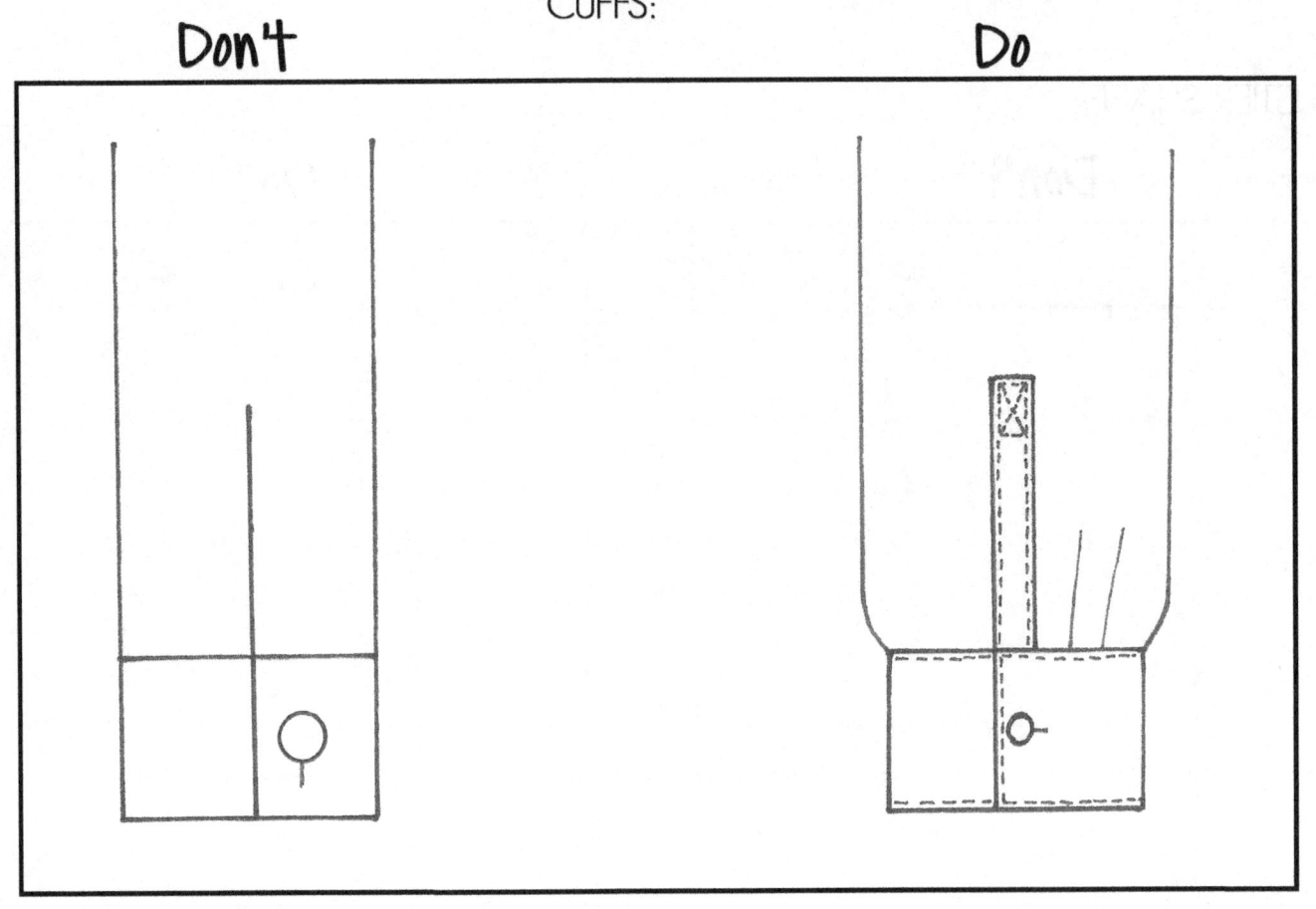

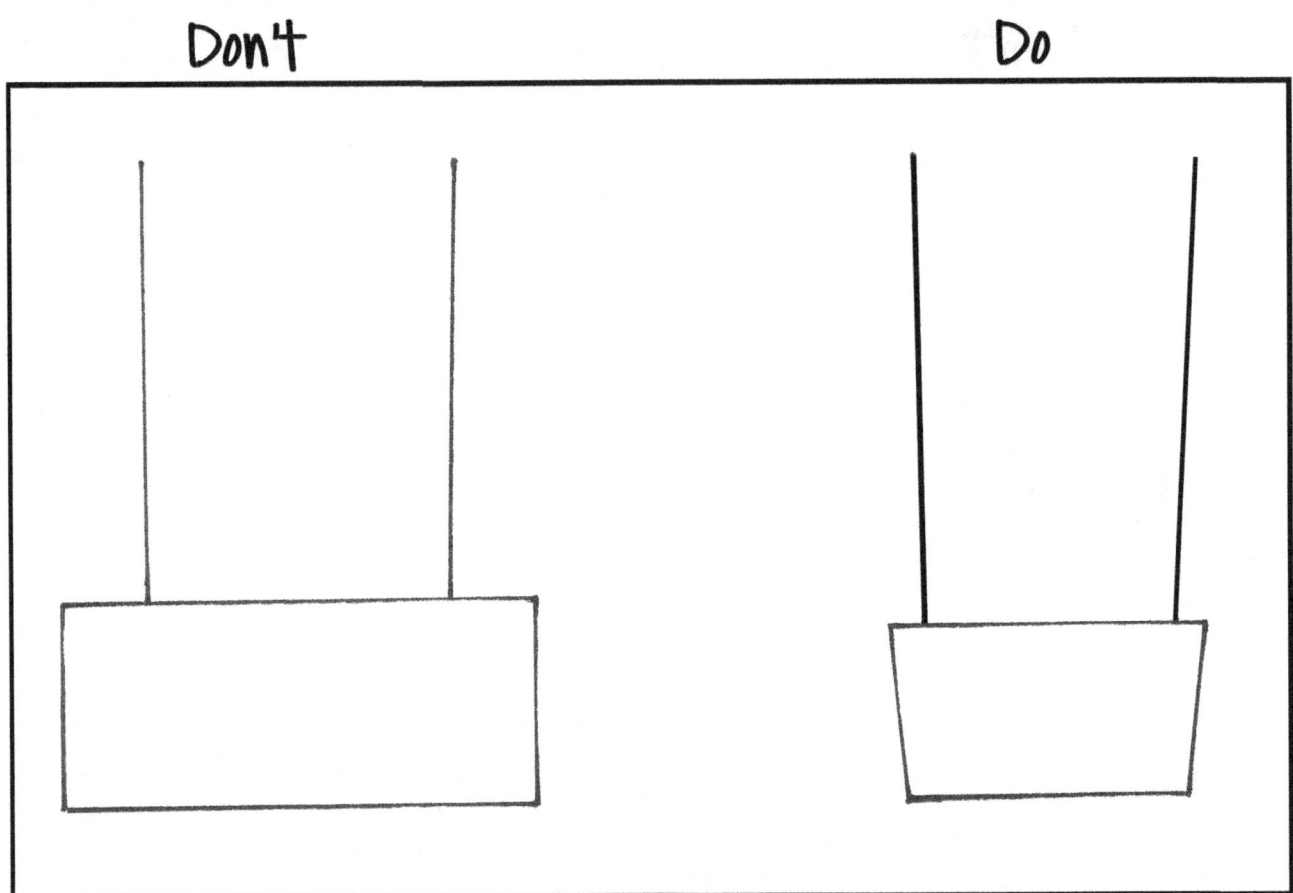

Don't   **Do**

Don't   **Do**

24.

T-Shirts
RIBBING

Don't

Do

Don't

Do

25.

Tops
RIBBING

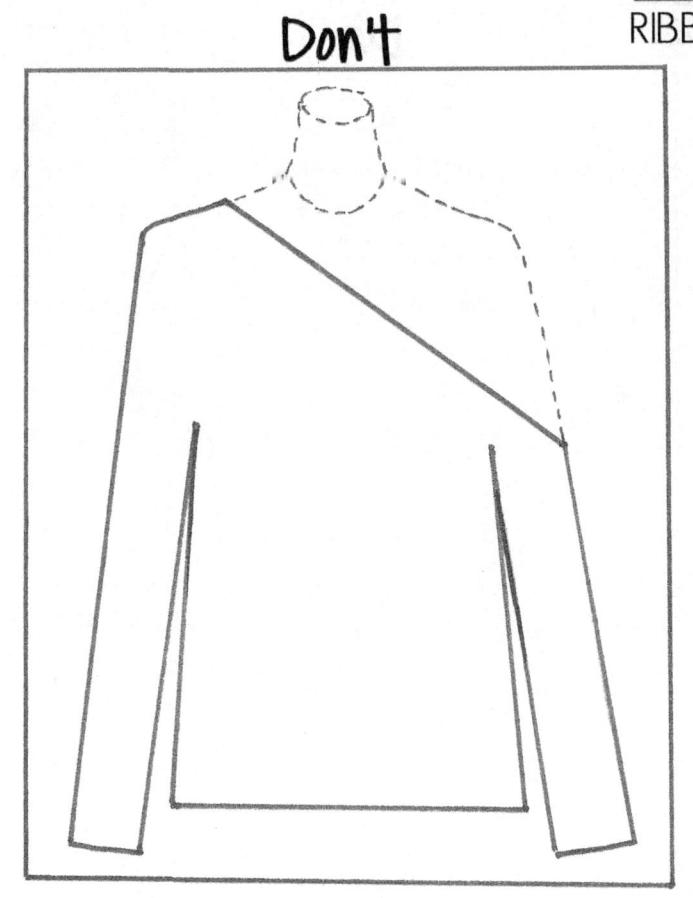

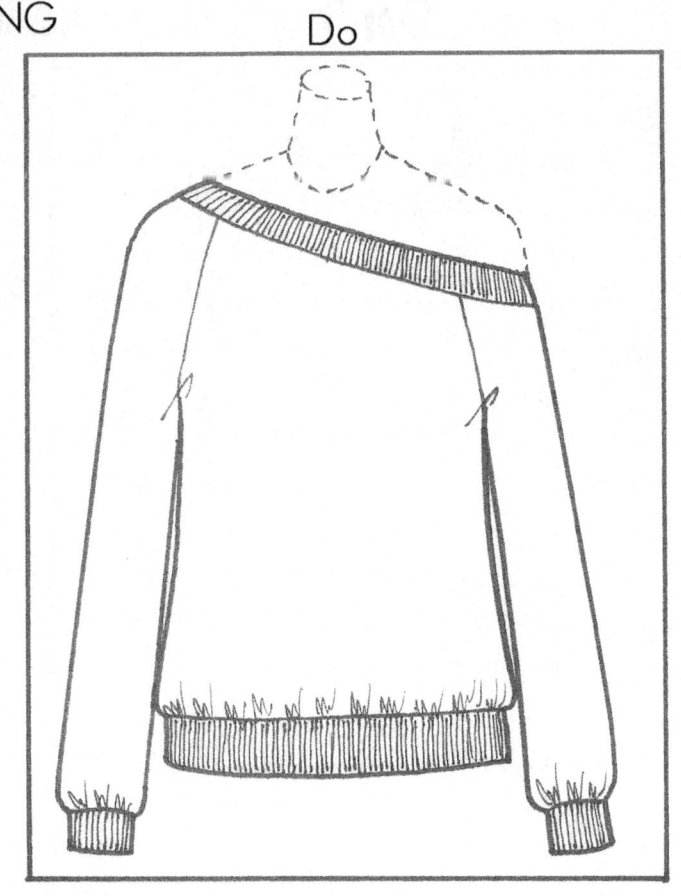

Don't

Do

GATHERS

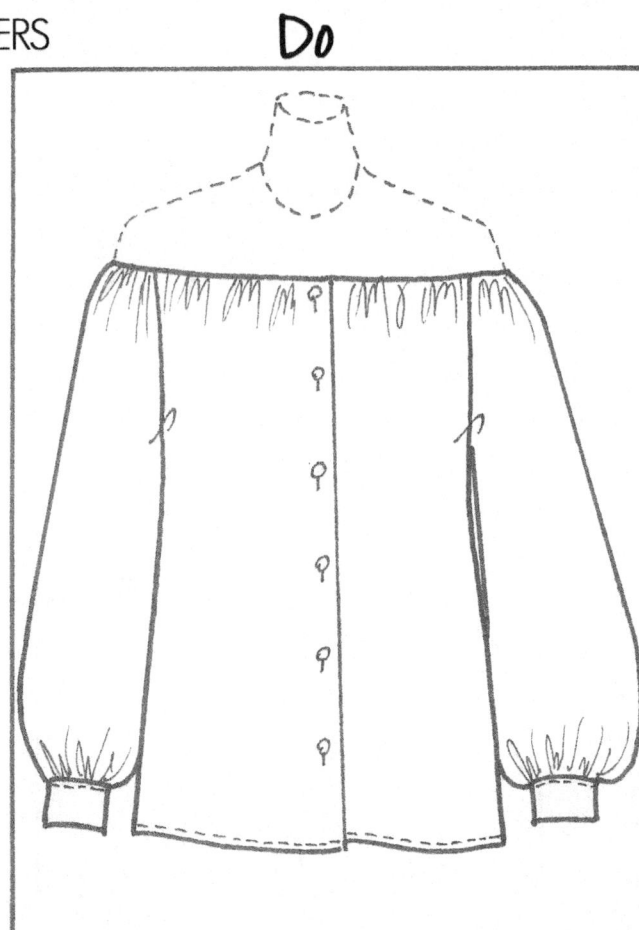

Don't

Do

26.

Tops
COWL DRAPE

Don't

Do

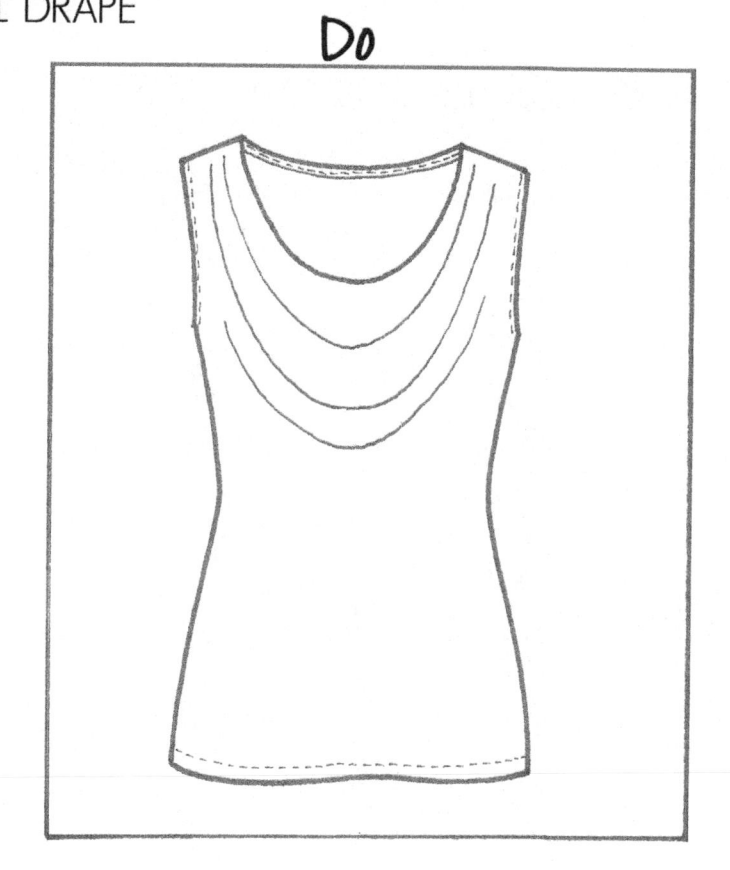

Don't

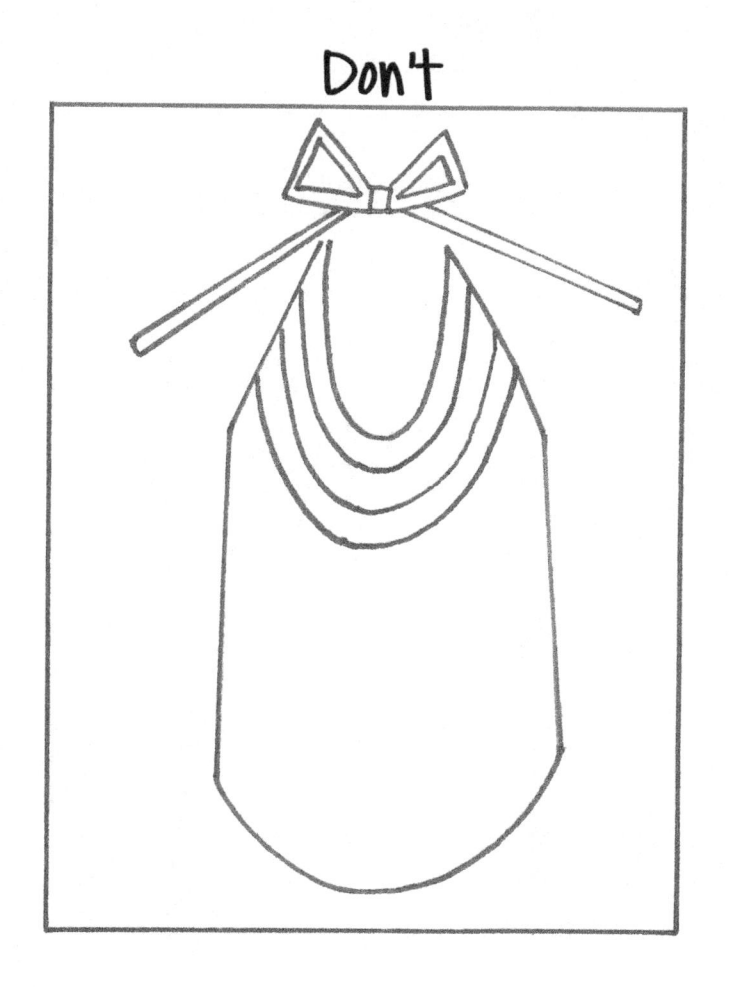

Do

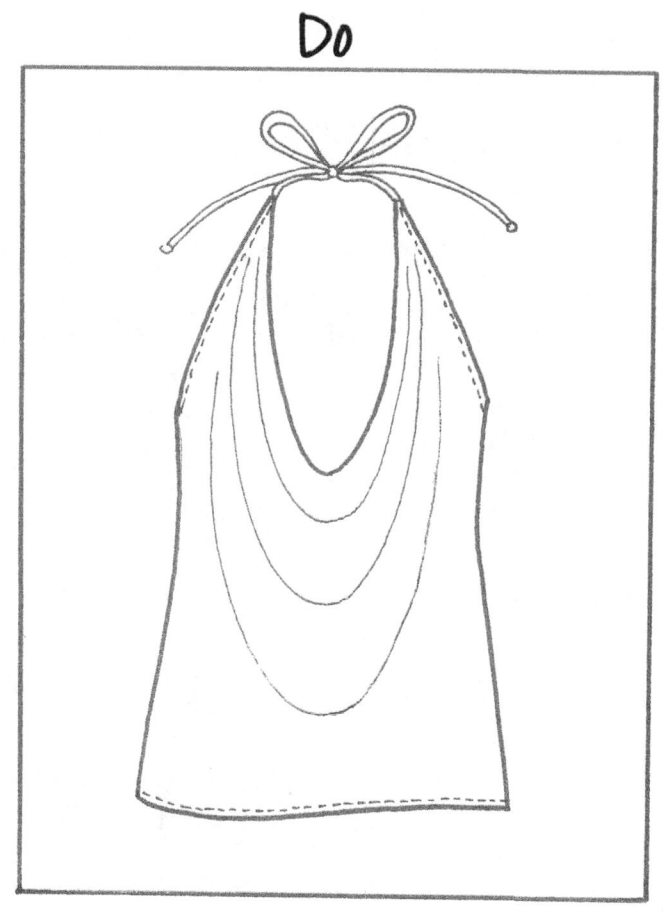

27.

TOPS
STITCHING

When necessary, DO NOT FORGET to include proper STITCHING:

WESTERN-STYLE COTTON SHIRT

KNIT HOODIE ZIP-UP JACKET

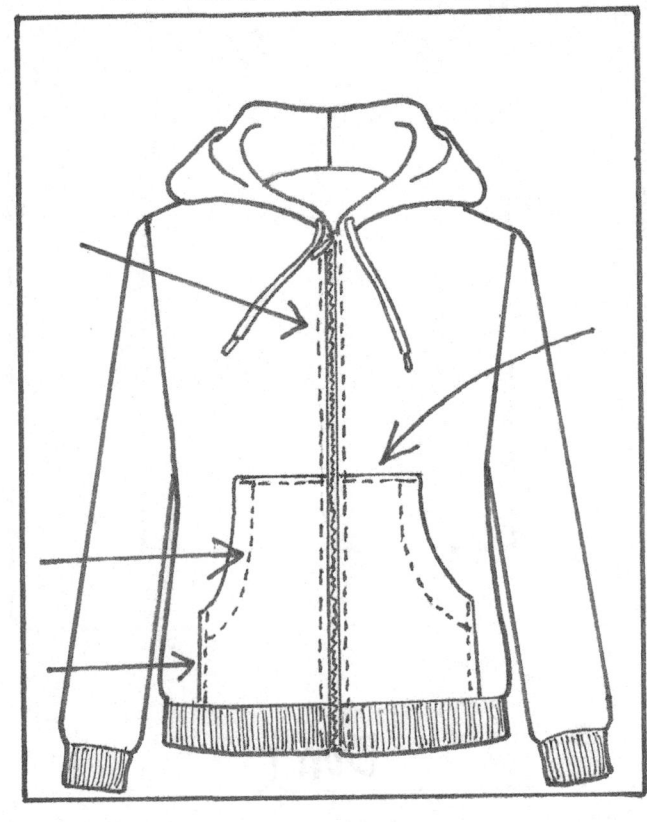

KNIT T-SHIRT

SILK BLOUSE

28.

DRESSES

Dresses
SEAMS

Don't | **Do** | **Don't** | **Do**

CF | CF | CF | CF

Don't | **Do** | **Don't** | **Do**

CB | CB | CF | CF

31.

Dresses

Don't
Do

RUFFLES

Don't
Do

GATHERS

32.

Dresses

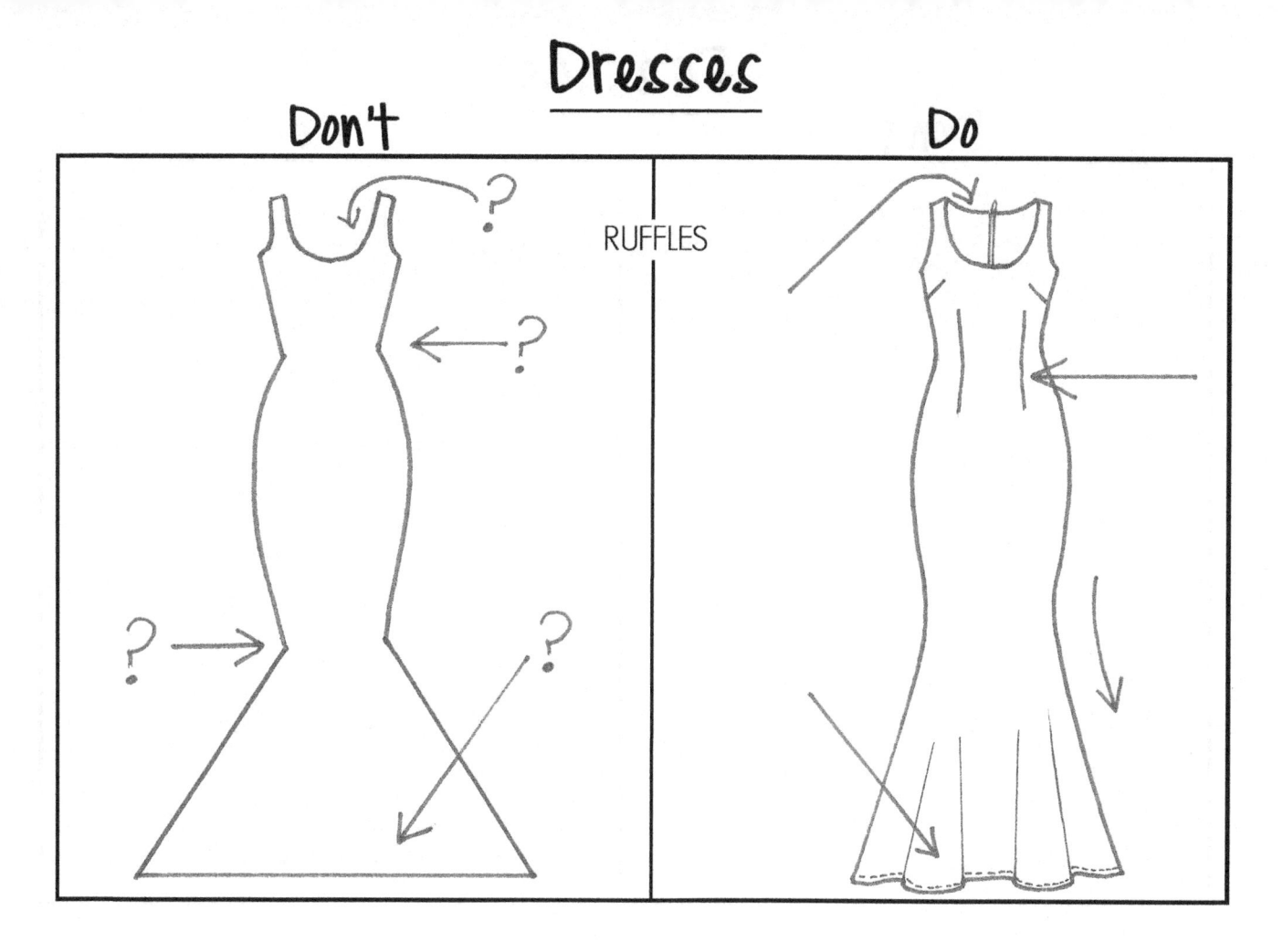

Don't   Do

RUFFLES

Don't   Do

GATHERS

Dresses

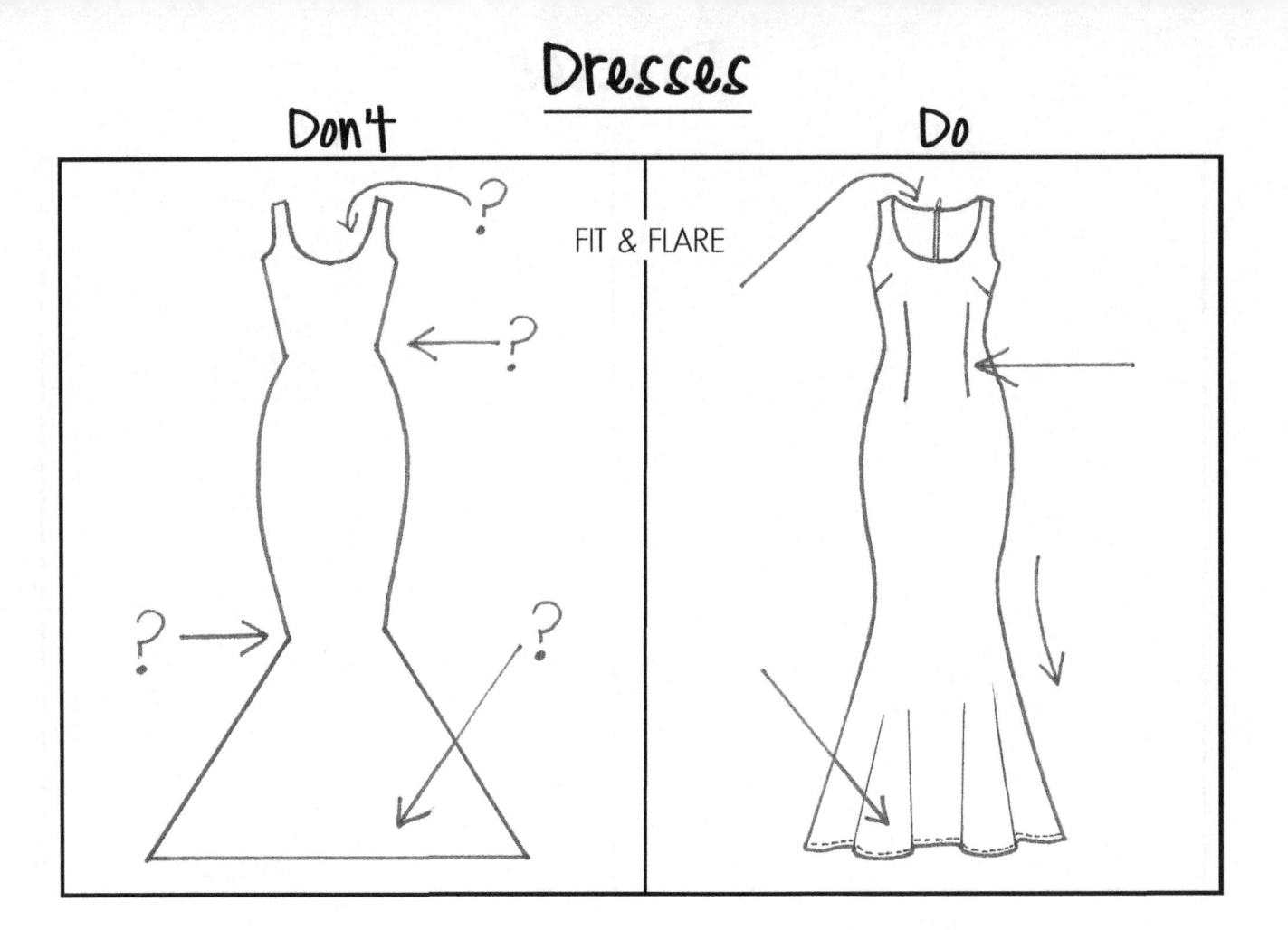

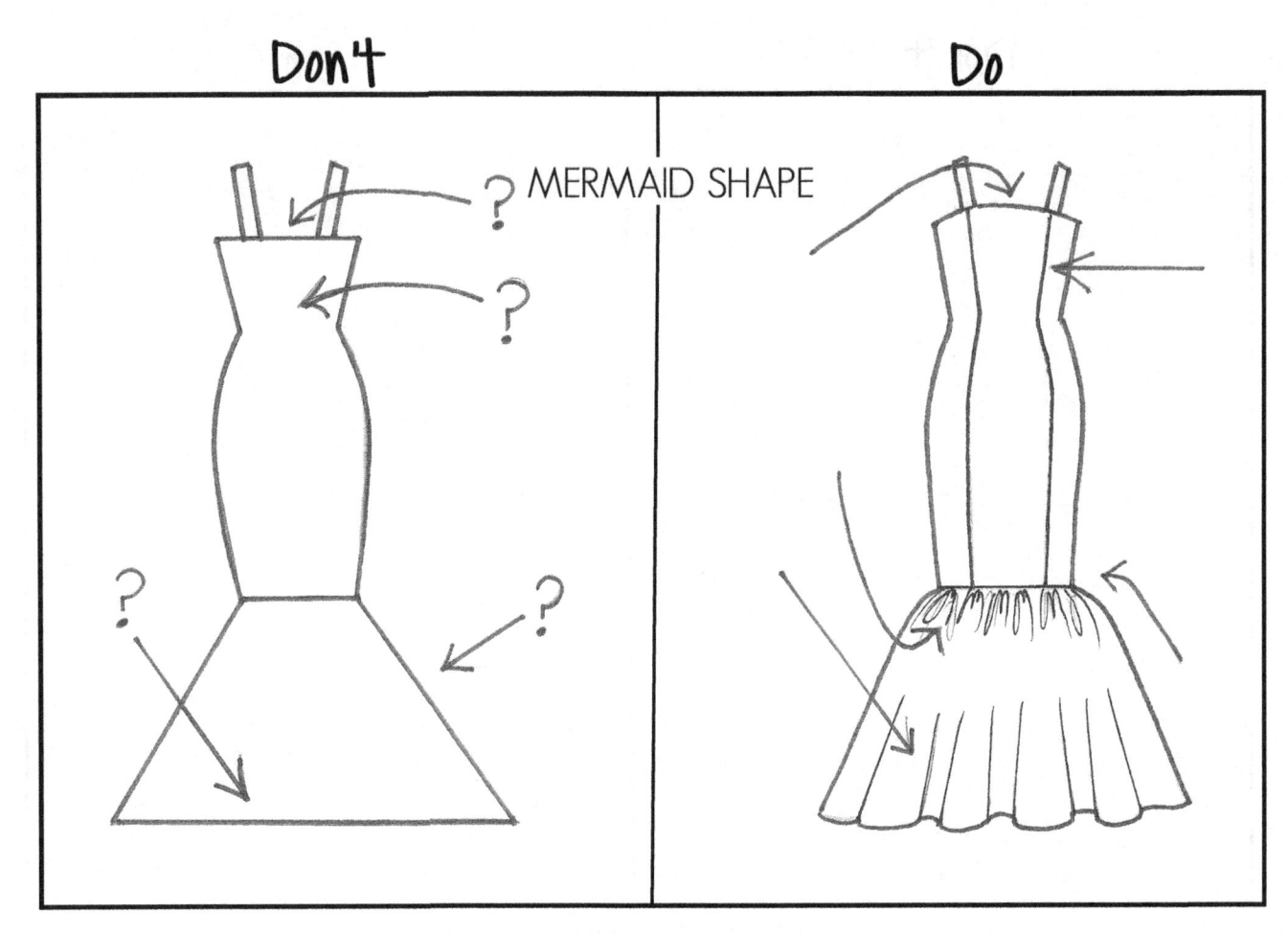

Don't | Do

FIT & FLARE

Don't | Do

MERMAID SHAPE

34.

JACKETS

Jackets
LAPELS & DARTS

Don't

Do

Don't

Do

37.

Jackets
LAPELS & DARTS

Don't

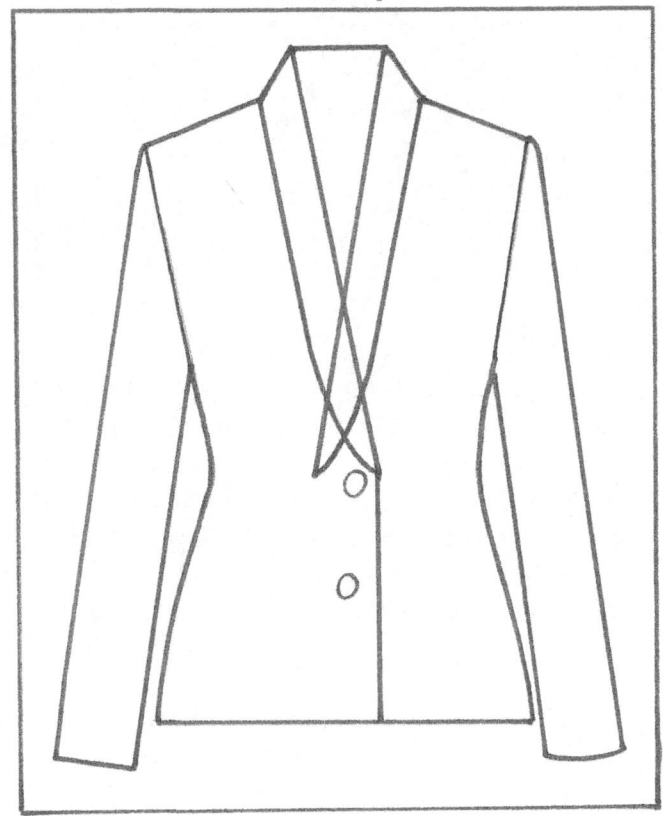

Do

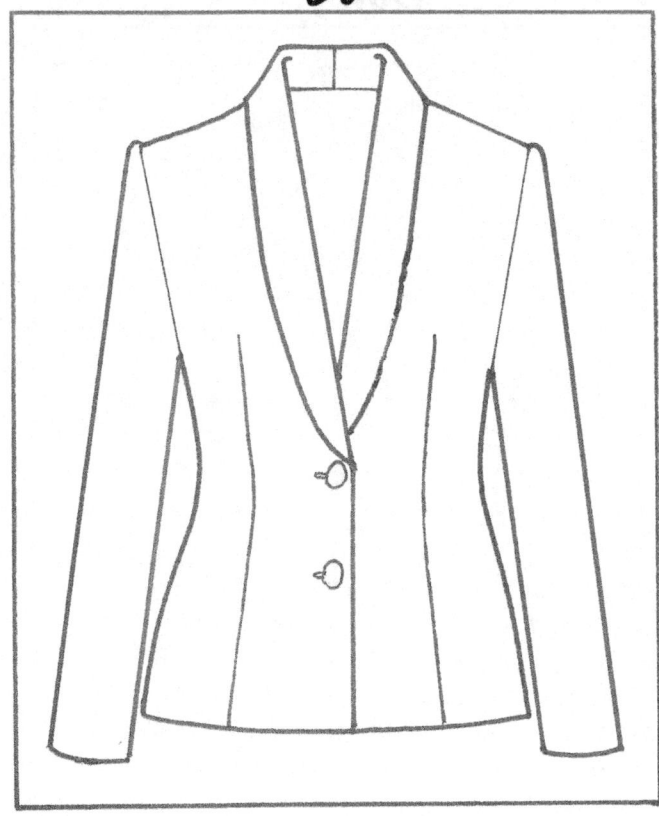

Don't

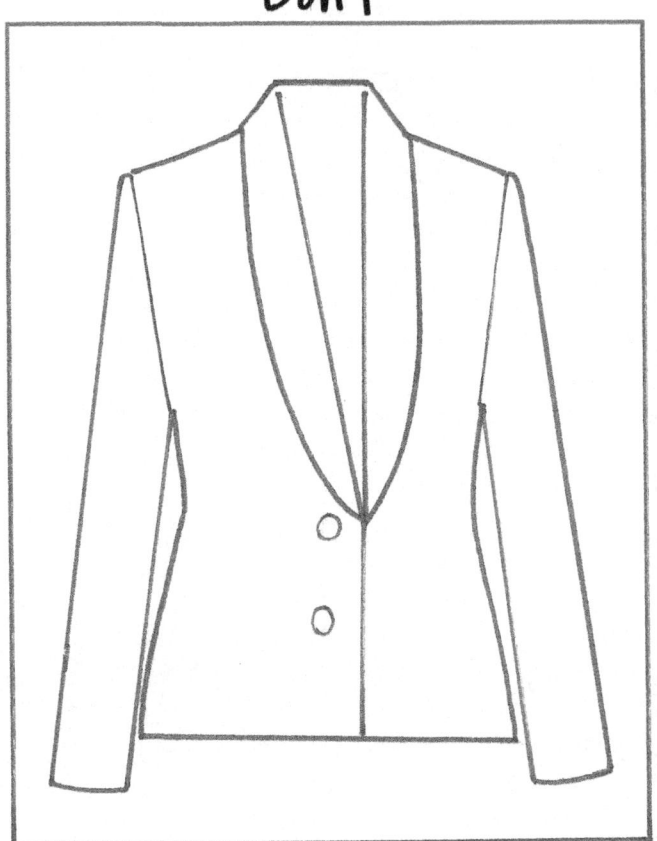

Do

38.

Jackets
SHAPE & PRINCESS SEAMS

Don't

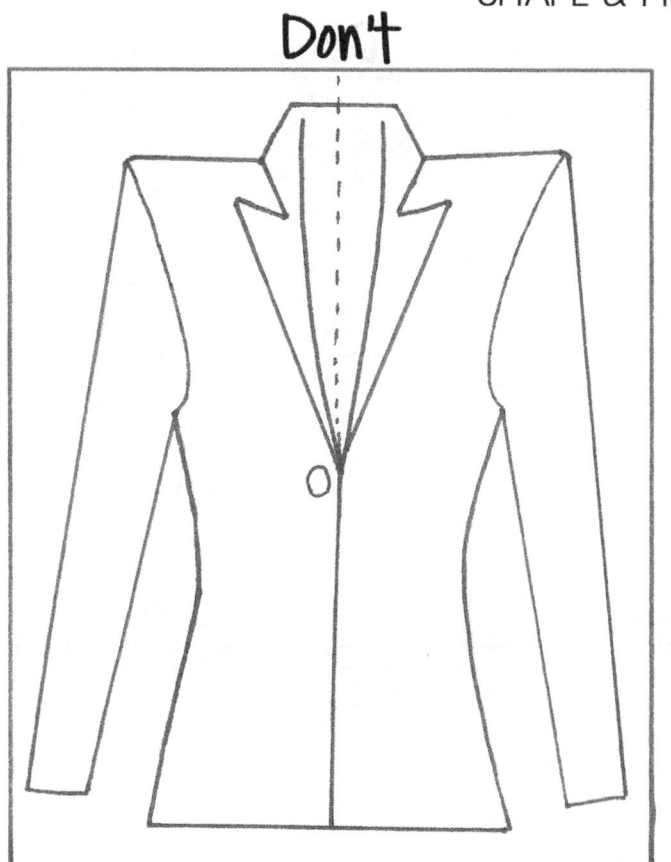

Do

DARTS & SEAMS

Don't

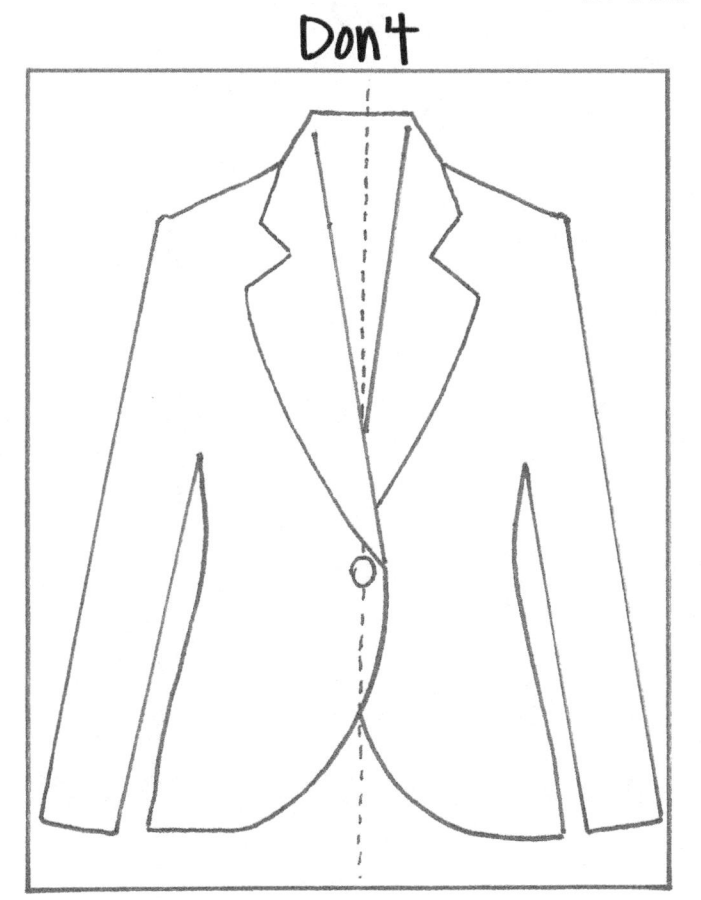

Do

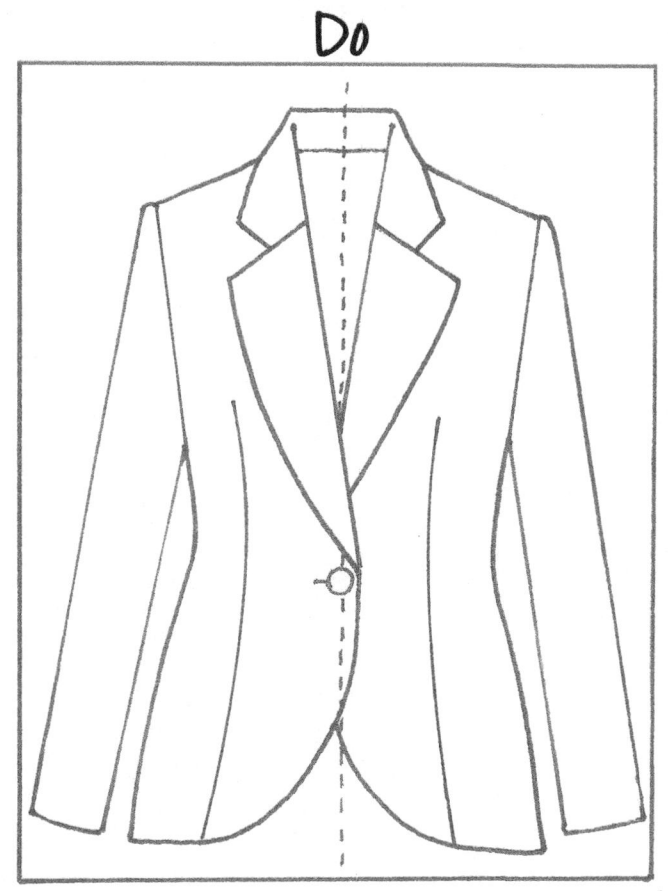

39.

Jackets
SHAPE

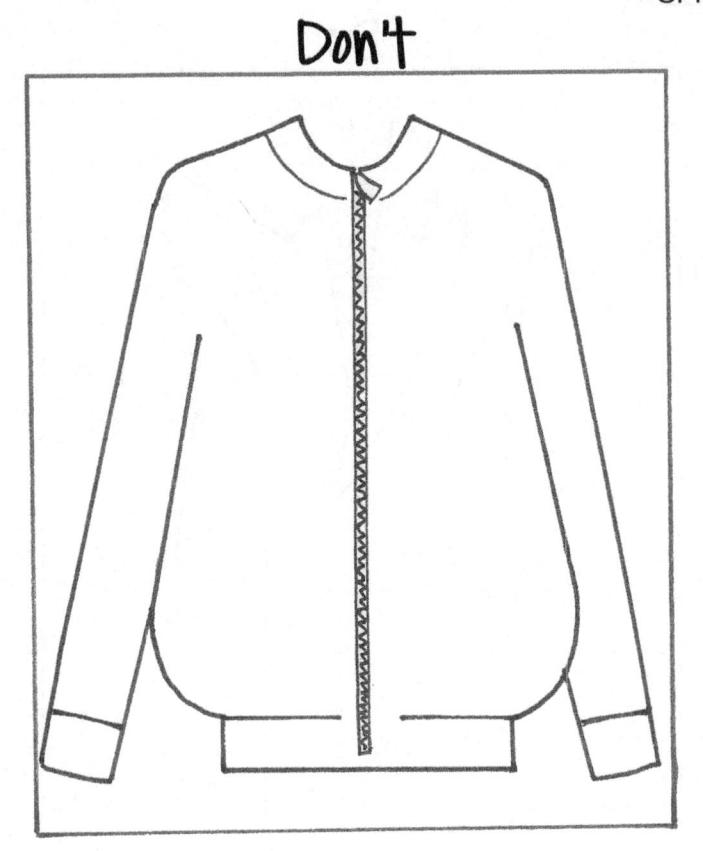

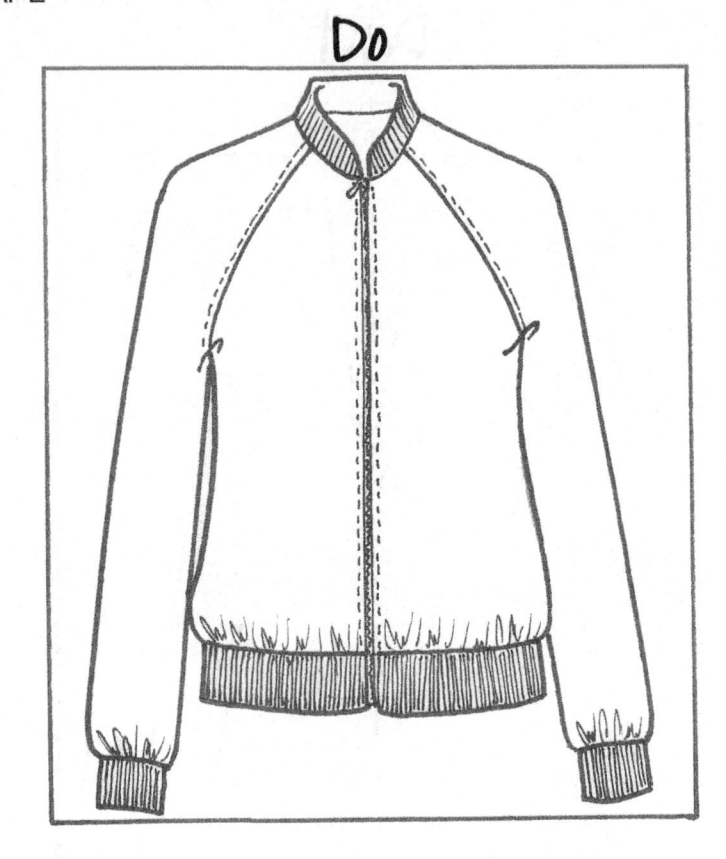

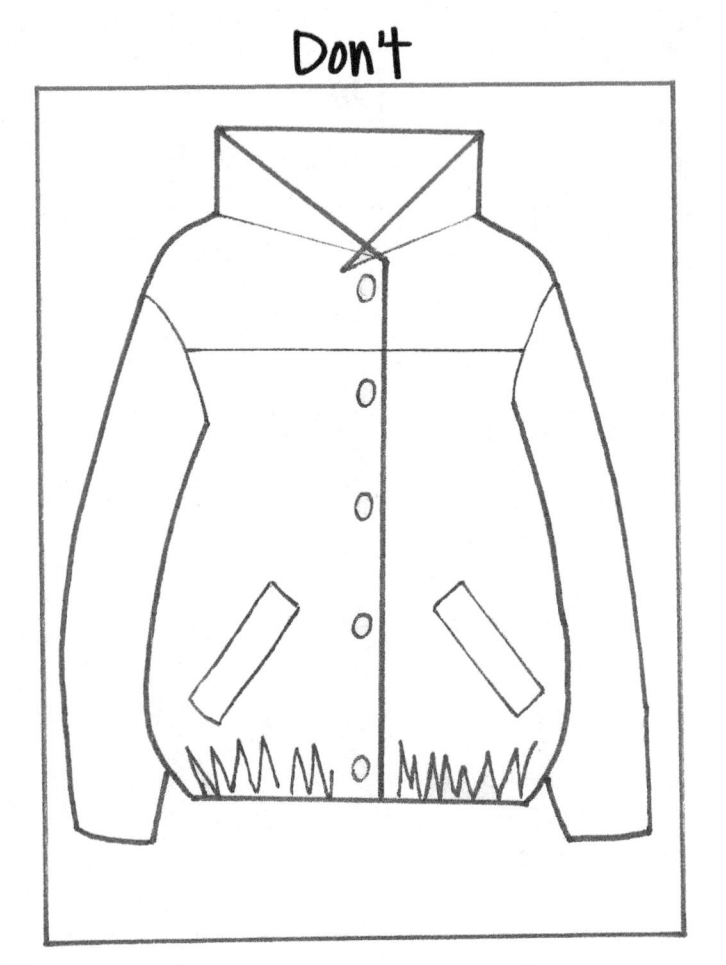

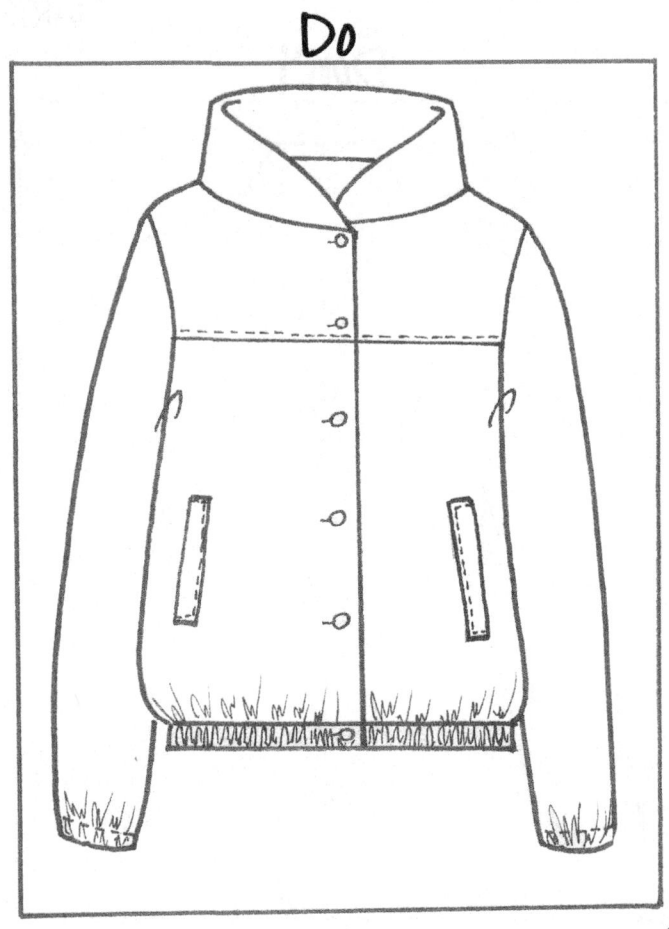

Don't

Do

Don't

Do

40.

Hoods

Don't	Do

Don't	Do

41.

Made in the USA
Middletown, DE
27 July 2023